A PICKWICK PORTRAIT GALLERY

Mr. Pickwick addresses the club.

A PICKWICK PORTRAIT GALLERY

FROM THE PENS OF DIVERS ADMIRERS
OF THE ILLUSTRIOUS MEMBERS
OF THE PICKWICK CLUB
THEIR FRIENDS AND
ENEMIES

KENNIKAT PRESS
Port Washington, N. Y./London

823.8
D548 p
1970

A PICKWICK PORTRAIT GALLERY

First published in 1936
Reissued in 1970 by Kennikat Press
Library of Congress Catalog Card No: 75-105822
ISBN 0-8046-1030-4

Manufactured by Taylor Publishing Company   Dallas, Texas

FOREWORD

THIS album of Pickwickian portraiture, the work of various and distinguished hands, has been planned and prepared by the publishers as a tribute to the "Pickwick" centenary, and as a memorial to the hundred years' association under which the names of Pickwick and of Chapman & Hall have come down the generations to the present day, inseparably hand in hand.

"Pickwick" has long since been the whole world's property, commercially no less than sentimentally; the life of copyright is short; and the day soon arrives when every market is open to the cherished freehold of the brain. But if ever a book was bound by ties of loyalty and gratitude to the memory of its original publishers, that book is "The Posthumous Papers of the Pickwick Club." It is true that the artist, Robert Seymour, was the first to hit upon the idea of a Cockney Sporting Club; but it was Edward Chapman, the publisher, who conceived the temperament and appearance of Samuel Pickwick himself; and it was Chapman & Hall's reader who suggested that the letter-press to accompany Seymour's plates should be entrusted to a brilliant young man whom he almost believed himself to have "discovered"—the newspaper reporter, Charles Dickens, just making his first appearance as a story-teller under the arresting pseudonym of "Boz." The young man was willing; the publishers had their own ideas; but were wise enough to adapt them to the author's fancy. In the quaint little bow-windowed office at 186 Strand, Chapman & Hall and Charles Dickens talked out their plans, and agreed with one another over terms. "Pickwick" was launched upon the world, to make the reputation of the author in a single season, and to lift the publishers straight into the leading ranks of their trade or profession. The day that "Pickwick" burst upon the world is a land-mark in the history of publishing. A hundred years have passed, and the popularity of that immortal work is still unimpugned and unimpugnable. . . .

Let us now praise famous men, and the builders who built far better than they knew! . . .

CHAPMAN & HALL LTD.

11 HENRIETTA STREET,
COVENT GARDEN.

March 31st, 1936.

CONTENTS

			page
	FOREWORD		7
I.	SAMUEL PICKWICK	by Alfred Noyes	13
II.	NATHANIEL WINKLE	by Ralph Straus	27
III.	AUGUSTUS SNODGRASS AND THE REV. MR. STIGGINS	by G. W. Stonier	41
IV.	MR. TUPMAN	by J. W. T. Ley	55
V.	SAMUEL WELLER	by John Betjeman	69
VI.	TONY WELLER	by Bransby Williams	83
VII.	JINGLE	by Alec Waugh	95
VIII.	MR. WARDLE	by Walter Dexter	105
IX.	MRS. BARDELL	by Beatrice Kean Seymour	121
X.	SERGEANT BUZFUZ	by Bernard Darwin	135
XI.	MESSRS. DODSON AND FOGG	by E. S. P. Haynes	149
XII.	BOB SAWYER	by J. Johnston Abraham	163
XIII.	THE FAT BOY	by Arthur Waugh	187
XIV	DR. SLAMMER	by Hugh Kingsmill	203
XV	DINGLEY DELL v. ALL-MUGGLETON CRICKET MATCH	by A. G. Macdonell	219
XVI	THE SMALLEST FRY	by James Agate	233

LIST OF ILLUSTRATIONS

Mr. Pickwick addresses the Club (*Seymour*)   *Frontispiece*

Mr. Winkle soothes the refractory steed (*Seymour*)   *Facing page* 28

Mr. Weller attacks the executive of Ipswich (Mr. Snodgrass in truly Christian spirit proceeded to take his coat off with the utmost deliberation) (*Phiz*) .   ,,   ,,   42

The Fat Boy awake on this occasion only (*Phiz*)   ,,   ,,   56

First appearance of Mr. Samuel Weller (*Phiz*)   ,,   ,,   70

The Valentine (*Phiz*)   ,,   ,,   84

Discovery of Jingle in the Fleet (*Phiz*)   ,,   ,,   96

Mr. Wardle and his friends under the influence of the salmon (*Phiz*)   ,,   ,,   106

Mrs. Bardell faints in Mr. Pickwick's arms (*Phiz*)   ,,   ,,   122

The Trial (*Phiz*)   ,,   ,,   136

Mr. Pickwick and Sam in the attorney's office (*Phiz*)   ,,   ,,   150

Conviviality at Bob Sawyer's (*Phiz*)   ,,   ,,   164

Mary and the Fat Boy (*Phiz*)   ,,   ,,   188

Doctor Slammer's defiance of Jingle (*Seymour*)   ,,   ,,   204

The cricket match at Muggleton (*Buss—suppressed plate*)   ,,   ,,   220

The Card Room at Bath (*Phiz*)   ,,   ,,   234

SAMUEL PICKWICK
By Alfred Noyes

I

IN the *Pickwick Papers* Dickens was still learning the secrets of his own craftsmanship. He had not yet found himself. The influence of Smollet was still perceptible, especially perhaps in the prison scenes. Jingle has at least a nodding acquaintance with the Gil Blas whom Dickens had encountered in that famous little garret of his childhood, among the battered old books and cobwebs. The author of *Pickwick* was an obscure young man who had been set the task of making a suitable text to accompany the work of a popular artist. He was not yet his own master or the master of his medium. Yet the book is as sure of immortality as any in the language.

This is chiefly due to the fact that several of the characters broke through all the restrictions, by simply coming to life, in the author's hands, and walking straight out of his pages into the world of living men and women. Adverse critics have found that the earlier pages of *Pickwick* have a certain crudity; and that there is, for the taste of the present day, a little too much of the hot, "reeking brandy and water" as a necessary ingredient in the Dickensian receipt for a comfortable evening by the fire. But consciously or unconsciously Dickens in these pages was really making use of a convention. Just as Stevenson's pirates called for rum, so did that lover of human cosiness, Mr. Pickwick, when he alighted at his inn, call for hot, steaming punch, with a dash of lemon in it. Drawn curtains and a blazing fire were part of the same symbolism, and, indeed, it might also be added that winter and snow outside were almost a part of it too. The little lighted room and the sense of the black night outside were àll a part of the technical convention whereby Dickens began to suggest something far more important—the necessity for friendship and kindliness and compassion in a world where winter's tooth was keen, and life was brief, and the night was long. Mr. Pickwick develops as the story proceeds, and before it had come to Christmas at Dingley Dell he had become just as much a real person and, in fact, just as much a public character as Mr. Gladstone. His views on a great many subjects were known or taken for granted. He was a personage who must have been recognised, as Mr. Gladstone used to be recognised, if he appeared in a public place; and, wherever he went, one feels that he would have been treated with consideration and respect.

Indeed, this is one of the most astonishing things about Mr. Pickwick. Other characters in fiction may strike the imagination and may force us to say "how true to life" or "how typical." But there are certain feelings which are almost always reserved for real persons and are usually not touched at all by characters in fiction. These are not necessarily the deepest feelings. Characters in fiction do very frequently move these. They move our affections, as in fact Mr. Pickwick does also. But there are curious little additions in Mr. Pickwick's case which belong essentially to biography rather than fiction. There are times when one feels that *Pickwick* should be placed somewhere near Boswell's *Johnson*, as one of the two greatest biographies in the language. One has a strange sense of personal respect for Mr. Pickwick, the kind of respect that we feel for Dr. Johnson, and a few other historical figures of decided and dogmatic but amiable views. Mr. Pickwick was, of course, gentler than Dr. Johnson. He approximated a little more closely to Goldsmith physically and in personal character. But he commanded more respect than Goldie, and in his indignation he could crush his followers almost as effectively as the great Doctor, without leaving the slightest ill-feeling after the event. His club, like most of the members of the Johnsonian circle, accepted correction at his hands as schoolboys accept it from a master whom they know to be both just and considerate.

It is difficult to think of any other character in fiction who imposes this peculiar respect upon the reader, at the very moment when he is making the reader smile at him. Don Quixote, in a more fantastic way, suggests a remote similarity, and Mr. Pickwick had his own quixotries; but the Knight of the Rueful Countenance is too remote from ordinary life to be compared with a creature so plump and rosily human. Mr. Pickwick is a highly respectable citizen, a sound Englishman, who, we feel, can be trusted to do the right thing and vote for the right cause in most political and moral crises. His moral indignation has its comic aspect—as Dickens shows us—but it was one of the triumphs of Dickens's genius that he was able to make us feel, at the same time, Mr. Pickwick's formidable capacity for righteous indignation and respect it. He may have been wheeled into the pound in a wheelbarrow, in the earlier part of the book, and we accept it with a smile as we accept the "frolic" mood of the earlier Johnson. Mr. Pickwick's indignation when he wakes and finds himself there is deliciously depicted. He will have damages for false imprisonment. He will prosecute!

"No, you won't," says his spiritual twin, Mr. Wardle.

"And why not, pray?" asks Mr. Pickwick, a little haughtily.

"Because," answers Mr. Wardle, "they might say something about cold punch."

The indignant stare of Mr. Pickwick slowly melts into a smile, which is Dickens's own inimitable way of asking all moralists everywhere "not to look too good." In some of these ways Mr. Pickwick is the most critical and universal of the numerous clan to which he belongs, in the works of Dickens. He is the most representative of that large family of benevolent, middle-aged, or elderly angels in gaiters through whose agency, on Christmas Eve, so many pleasant things—"Dickensian things"—happen to stray tramps, to tired little waifs and strays, and even to the liar and the cheat when they are really down upon their luck.

One would like to know where Dickens discovered his model for the part; and whether, in the early stages of his own career—the Copperfield stages—he had ever encountered that twinkling kindness. One hopes that it may have been so. There is at least one representative of the Pickwick family in almost every story that Dickens wrote, and they are all tender-hearted and somewhat rotund in figure. One feels sure that they all have plump little gold watches in their fobs of the most solid and reliable make, and that they all have some difficulty in extracting them, after the cordial hospitality which they dispense to themselves as well as to others. There are the Cheeryble brothers in *Nicholas Nickleby*; there is Mr. Lorry in *A Tale of Two Cities*; there is "my guardian," one of the most lovable of them all, in *Bleak House*. In the *Pickwick Papers* itself—as was said above—there is Mr. Pickwick's spiritual twin, Mr.

Wardle. He is the country mouse or squire of the family, while Mr. Pickwick is the town mouse and in some ways more elegant. When somebody begs Mr. Wardle's pardon one regrets to observe that he replies "granted." But his Christmas at Dingley Dell has all the warmth and cordiality of Mr. Pickwick's own glowing heart.

In Mr. Pickwick himself, however, there are characteristics of a wider range. Indeed, in the early chapters of *Pickwick* there are indications that, if he had chosen to do so, Dickens might have developed an entirely different manner and, with less attention to the creation of character, might have given us great broad satirical cartoons of the life of the nineteenth century, on a Rabelaisian scale, though still in the clean Dickensian spirit. Nobody can read the extract from the transactions of the Pickwick Club in the first chapter of the book without feeling that the lambent light of Dickens's humour is playing around something much larger than its pretended subject. The detail is cruder, because he is not thinking so much of that. The Parliamentary correspondent has made good use of his observations in another place, when he makes Mr. Blotton of Aldgate rise to order and ask:

" 'Did the honourable Pickwickian allude to him?' (*Cries of 'order,' 'chair,' 'yes,' 'no,' 'go on,' 'leave off,' etc.*)

"Mr. Pickwick would not put up to be put down by clamour. He *had* alluded to the honourable gentleman (*great excitement*).

"Mr. Blotton would only say then, that he repelled the hon. gent.'s false and scurrilous accusation with profound contempt (*great cheering*). The hon. gent. was a humbug. (*Immense confusion, and loud cries of 'chair' and 'order.'*)

"Mr. A. Snodgrass rose to order. He threw himself upon

18

the chair. (*Hear!*) He wished to know whether this disgraceful contest between two members of that club should
be allowed to continue. (*Hear! Hear!*)

"The Chairman was quite sure the hon. Pickwickian
would withdraw the expression he had just made use of.

"Mr. Blotton, with all possible respect for the chair,
was quite sure he would not.

"The Chairman felt it his imperative duty to demand of
the hon. gent. whether he had used the expression which
had just escaped him, in a common sense.

"Mr. Blotton had no hesitation in saying that he had
not—he had used the word in a Pickwickian sense. (*Hear!
Hear!*) He was bound to acknowledge that, personally, he
entertained the highest regard and esteem for the honourable gentleman; he had merely considered him a humbug
in the Pickwickian point of view. (*Hear! Hear!*)

"Mr. Pickwick felt much gratified by the fair, candid
and full explanation of his honourable friend. He begged it
to be at once understood that his own observations had
been merely intended to have a Pickwickian construction.
(*Cheers.*)"

The amazing thing about this piece of broad satire is
that it is as true to its real object to-day as it was when it
was written a hundred years ago. If we compare it to-day
with any of the Parliamentary reports of a minor tempest
in the House it will be observed that it hits off the exact
phrasing, the gesture, the pose, the manner of threatening,
the failure of the threat, the face-saving withdrawals on
both sides, and the subsequent absurd reconciliations of the
absurd process to a nicety. The "gratification" of Mr.
Pickwick in all this has been the "gratification" of innumerable politicians and statesmen since his day. But

the Mother of Parliaments is not the only target in those opening pages. "There sat the man who had traced to their source the mighty ponds of Hampstead, and agitated the scientific world with his theory of Tittlebats."

Both of these veins, the political and the scientific, were developed in later chapters: the political in the account of the Eatanswill election, and the scientific in the antiquarian researches of Mr. Pickwick and those remarkable memoranda on all kinds of subjects, from cart-horses to ancient inscriptions, which he was so fond of jotting down in his note-book. This insatiable eagerness of Mr. Pickwick for information is yet another link between him and Dr. Johnson, who frequently urged Boswell to report all manner of strange items to him.

But, as the book developed, the characters themselves took the law into their own hands. Mr. Pickwick mellowed and, from being merely a subject of good-natured mirth, revealed himself as the very soul of good-nature and a man to be loved. The protective devotion of Sam Weller to Mr. Pickwick is depicted with some of the truest touches of Dickens's genius. The tender heart has no armour, and the son of the mean streets recognises it, and appoints himself as the guardian and guide of his own master against the wickedness of the world.

The turning-point in the book and the turning-point in the art of Dickens is the moment when Mr. Pickwick, in prison, is induced by compassion for the persecutor who brought him there, to abandon his sturdy resolution, and set both his persecutor and himself free. We may smile at the absurd tangle into which Mr. Pickwick had been entrapped; but, at the same time, Dickens makes us feel that he had found the master-key to the debtors' prison, and with that same key he unlocked the hearts of the English-speaking world.

The reader derives considerable satisfaction, nevertheless, from the fact that Mr. Pickwick's good-nature is not extended so far as to cover the sins of Messrs. Dodson and Fogg. There are few scenes in fiction where cool impertinence and the hot anger of a good man, together with the comedy that always accompanies lack of self-control, are so justly and delightfully depicted. The nauseating hypocrisy of the two rascally lawyers is more subtly drawn, and truer to life, than that of Uriah Heep or Pecksniff; and their attempt to converse with Mr. Pickwick on equal terms, or rather to treat him as one whose former conduct they were ready to overlook, is met by a snub as crushing as any uttered by that other Samuel. Mr. Dodson, preparing to receive the costs of the Bardell case from Mr. Pickwick, affably remarks:

"I don't think you are looking quite so stout as when I had the pleasure of seeing you last, Mr. Pickwick."

"Possibly not, sir," replied Mr. Pickwick, who had been flashing forth looks of fierce indignation, without producing the smallest effect on either of the sharp practitioners; "I believe I am not, sir. I have been persecuted and annoyed by scoundrels, of late, sir."

Perker coughed violently, and asked Mr. Pickwick whether he wouldn't like to look at the morning paper.

The whole of this scene is masterly; and it culminates in a comic symphony, in which every participant is perfect, and every note precisely right.

"*Good* morning, Mr. Pickwick," said Fogg. So saying, he put his umbrella under his arm, drew off his right glove, and extended the hand of reconciliation to that most indignant gentleman: who thereupon, thrust his hands beneath his coat tails and eyed the attorney with looks of scornful amazement.

The apprehensive interjections of Mr. Pickwick's good little representative, Mr. Perker, are as exquisitely touched in as the mixed feelings and strictly legal attitude of the rascals:

"My dear sir, pray let the matter rest where it is . . . Mr. Pickwick, I beg!" cries the nervous Mr. Perker.

"Take care, sir," said Dodson, intrenched behind Fogg. "Let him assault you, Mr. Fogg; don't return it on any account. . . ."

And then the final outburst from Mr. Pickwick— "a well-matched pair of mean, rascally, pettifogging robbers!"

"There!" said Perker in a most conciliatory tone. "My dear sirs, he has said all he has to say. Now pray go. Lowten, *is* that door open?"

Mr. Lowten, with a distant giggle, replied in the affirmative.

"There—there—good morning—good morning, now pray, my dear sirs . . . " cried the little man, pushing Dodson and Fogg, nothing loath, out of the office; "this way, my dear sirs—now pray don't prolong this—dear me — Mr. Lowten — the door, sir — why don't you attend?" . . .

"Robbers," cried Mr. Pickwick, running to the stair-head, as the two attorneys descended. . . .

"Robbers!" shouted Mr. Pickwick, breaking from Lowten and Perker, and thrusting his head out of the staircase window.

Then, walking quietly back into the office, he declared

that he had now removed a great weight from his mind, and that he felt perfectly comfortable and happy.

What modern psychological exponent of the danger of suppressed emotions could better this humorous illustration of beneficent relief? There is not a touch of caricature in it, from beginning to end, beyond what Nature herself will constantly impose upon her children. But the real triumph—which only a very great genius could achieve— is in making us feel the intrinsic goodness and humour of a character at whom we are forced to smile. Shakespeare might make us feel something like an amused sympathy for that fat rogue, Falstaff; but no one, I think, before Dickens, had so hit off the divine incongruity of things as to make his readers profoundly respect a character so absurdly human as Mr. Samuel Pickwick, at the very moment when he moved their laughter most forcibly. Even Mr. Perker, when the scene was over, was convulsed for a considerable time before he was able to speak; but, as soon as he recovered, the "many professions of friendship and esteem" were undoubtedly mutual.

In this scene, in fact, as in many others, especially in the second half of the work, Mr. Pickwick, although a figure of comedy, ceases to be the butt. At the beginning he was a figure in whom the sham conventions of political institutions, scientific bodies, and travellers with note-books were to be held up to ridicule. He developed into a chivalrous pilgrim, a very touchstone of truth, in contact wherewith charlatans were exposed and impostors occasionally became ashamed of themselves and were converted. He supplies, in fact, an answer to at least one short-sighted criticism of Dickens, upon which Mr. Andrew Lang made the following very just comment:

"People say that Dickens 'could not draw a gentleman.' Except in the heraldic sense, Mr. Pickwick is as much a gentleman as the Baron Bradwardine." It must be remembered, too, that Pickwick was created by a youth of twenty-three, whose experience of the world had not hitherto been exactly helpful in these respects. The fine qualities that he depicted, the courtesy, the courage, the kindliness, were those that appealed to his own nature. It is perfectly true, as Taine remarked, that we need no biography of a writer who so clearly reveals himself in his works; and indeed Mr. Pickwick does actually confute one of the more recent biographers on a very important point indeed. The biographer in question, Mr. Hugh Kingsmill, is a writer who very often has interesting and original things to say, but he surely slips into an amusing pit-fall when (illustrating what he supposes to be the laxity of Dickens's morals) he suggests that "like Mr. Pickwick" at the White Horse Dickens himself must "furtively" have turned the handles of many bedroom doors! The whole point of the episode, of course, was that Mr. Pickwick, in a panic of Victorian modesty, was desperately trying to discover his own room, and to escape from a most innocent and accidental encounter with an equally panic-stricken and elderly spinster of the most acidulated aspect imaginable.

It is perfectly true that Mr. Pickwick has a liking for a pretty face. But he is proof against all modern psycho-analysis. Nothing could be healthier and more normal. Mr. Andrew Lang probably comes nearest to the truth about him, when—in answer to the question why Mr. Pickwick had never married—he suggests that he had loved someone but never proposed, seeing that the object of his choice, as he would have said, "loved another." In some indefinable way, without any direct hint, Dickens contrives to give Mr. Pickwick, at the close of the book, something of the lonely sadness which he gave to "my guardian" in *Bleak House*. Mr. Pickwick is the guardian of the happiness of others. He dances at their weddings; he gives presents to the brides; he is godfather to their children. It is with a wedding that he celebrates his final house-warming, when he decides to abandon his travels and settle down at Dulwich. His new house, in which he is to grow old, might well make him exclaim with more truth than on any former occasion "this is indeed comfort."

"Everything was so beautiful, so compact, so neat, and in such exquisite taste." But there was one memory lacking; and the sentence in which we are told of his growing a little infirm nowadays, and going alone to look at the Dulwich gallery, would have a touch of sadness in it, if we did not know that, from time to time, his heart was warmed by the happiness of young people, under his own roof, the happiness of others, which "had ever been the chief pleasure of his life." Every year, moreover, he goes to Dingley Dell, attended by the faithful Sam, between whom and his master there exists a steady "attachment which nothing but death will terminate."

Mr. Pickwick's own speech, at the dissolution of the Pickwick Club, in a very few sentences sums up the development of his own character and the influence which it has had for good on all sorts and conditions of men. Beginning, as it seemed, with "a frivolous pursuit of novelty," it gradually reveals a new world of humour and compassion.

"Nearly the whole of my previous life," he says,

"having been devoted to business and the pursuit of wealth, numerous scenes of which I had no previous conception have dawned upon me—I hope to the enlargement of my mind and the improvement of my understanding." How many generations of his readers must echo this ! And again —was not Dickens himself speaking in the last sentences of Mr. Pickwick's farewell speech :

"If I have done but little good, I trust I have done less harm, and that none of my adventures will be other than a source of amusing and pleasant recollections to me in the decline of life. God bless you all !"

Whatever temptations there may be for the contemporary mind to read things into the life of Dickens that are not there, and to illustrate them from adventures of Mr. Pickwick that never happened, essential goodness remains essential goodness; and Dickens, however unfashionable the word may be at the moment, was essentially a good man. Deceit and disloyalty were essentially alien to him. If Mr. Pickwick illustrated anything in his career, it was this truth and loyalty; and it was for this reason that when Mr. Pickwick filled and drained his last toast, his friends "rose with one accord, and pledged him from their hearts."

NATHANIEL WINKLE

By Ralph Straus

II

APART altogether from the not inconsiderable part he plays in the various adventures that come the way of the Pickwickians, Mr. Nathaniel Winkle has an interest for us that is peculiarly his own, for it is he alone who can be said to lend any support to the odd contention, made sometimes even to-day, that *The Posthumous Papers of the Pickwick Club* was Robert Seymour's rather than Charles Dickens's invention.

In 1836 Seymour was enjoying a fair reputation. For the last fifteen or twenty years his comic, and generally sporting, sketches had been regularly appearing in all kinds of publications. In particular there had been issued in 1833 a little book called *Maxims and Hints for an Angler,* which professed to be a reprint of the Minutes of the Common Place Book of the Houghton Fishing Club. In some of the plates of this book you will find a fat bespectacled old boy who, it is true, bears some slight resemblance to the Mr. Pickwick that we know. Here, too, you may see a long thin gentleman who is not unlike Mr. Jingle and a cock-aded servant who might be a distant relation of Mr. Sam Weller. Again, in a series of lithographs issued two years later by Seymour and called *New Readings of Old Authors,* you may meet a fat old boy and a long thin man. They were, in point of fact, two of the artist's favourite stock figures. It is hardly surprising to hear that in the same year he was toying with the idea of illustrating the Chronicles of a Nimrod Club which should relate the comic mis-

Mr. Winkle soothes the refractory steed.

adventures of some vainglorious and unskilful Cockney "sportsman." The story goes that several sketches were prepared and shown to Theodore Hook as a possible collaborator. Hook found himself unable or unwilling to provide the necessary letterpress, and Seymour thereupon approached Edward Chapman, who, after one or two unsuccessful attempts to find a suitable author, offered a commission to "Boz."

Dickens's reply is well-known, "I objected," he was explaining to the world in 1847, "on consideration, that although born and partly bred in the country, I was no great sportsman . . . that the idea was not novel, and had been already much used; that it would be infinitely better for the plates to arise naturally out of the text, and that I should like to take my own way . . . I connected Mr. Pickwick with a club because of the original suggestion, and I put in Mr. Winkle expressly for the use of Mr. Seymour." No explanation, you would think, could be simpler. Unfortunately the artist's suicide after a very few *Pickwick* plates had appeared was said (by his family) to be due to acute disappointment, not to say anger, at an idea of his own being coolly appropriated by a pushing young writer.

All of which, I suppose, is not in these days a matter of much importance, but it ought to be mentioned in any paper which deals with a "sportsman" of the type which the ill-fated Seymour had in mind. Mr. Nathaniel Winkle, we may believe, is no Cockney—Birmingham, presumably, was his birthplace—but he probably conforms fairly closely to Seymour's original conception. He is a good, if singularly stupid, young fellow with one particular weakness: a desire, the natural desire of a timid

man, to "shine" in the various and supposedly dangerous
fields of sport. He cannot avoid boasting, though he would
prefer the boast by inference to anything like the lie direct,
and, as is only meet, he is badly shown up. Yet because,
even at his stupidest moments, there is nothing of the
vulgar cad about him, you can never dislike Mr. Winkle.
You laugh at his misfortunes, moreover, with an easy
conscience, for you realise that no real harm is being done
and are comfortably convinced that sooner or later he will
be mending his silly ways.

These misfortunes, you will remember, begin at the
very moment when the Pickwickians are setting out to
explore the world, for their cabman dashes "the whole
temporary supply of breath" out of his body. This,
admittedly, might happen to anybody, but it soon becomes clear that Mr. Winkle is not going to be let down
too lightly. In Rochester that particularly fine evening
suit of his—and you are not to forget that he and no other
was its designer: the Club Uniform, no less—is loaned,
without its owner's knowledge, to Mr. Jingle, whose
behaviour at public assemblies is not perhaps all that it
should be. The "warlike" Dr. Slammer conceives himself
to have been grossly insulted by the wearer of the suit, and
issues a challenge to its owner.

What is the poor man to do? He has no recollection of
ever having worn the suit in public, but too much wine,
of course, often deadens the memory. On the previous
evening he *may* have behaved in the most objectionable
way: in just the kind of way, perhaps, that "sportsmen"
in their cups might be expected to behave, and so, for the
sake of his reputation with his fellow-Pickwickians, he
comes to "the gloomy and dreadful resolve" to accept the

challenge. But what a position for a man of peace, even though he believes that pistols are "seldom loaded with ball," to find himself in! To add to his miseries, too, the usually amiable Snodgrass appears to regard each monstrous step in the preliminary proceedings as the merest matter of course. (But, as Dickens slyly observes, it is extraordinary how cool any party but the principals can be in such cases.)

It is not difficult to envisage a Winkle–Slammerian duel. Nobody, I feel, would have been killed, though one, or both, of the seconds might have been badly hurt. Luckily Dr. Slammer is not too angry, or too short-sighted, to see that his opponent is not the man who had so scandalously insulted him, and all is well.

Not, however, for any length of time, for soon enough the question of transport from Rochester has arisen. A coach's accommodation is limited, and not all the Pickwickians can find seats. But why worry? Naturally a sportsman like Winkle will go on horseback. He is invited to do so. It may be doubted whether he had ever sat on the back of even the smallest Shetland pony yet foaled, but how can he refuse? "I should enjoy it, of all things," says he, and forthwith and most valorously attempts to mount —on the wrong side. Even when instructed how to gain his seat, he is not strikingly successful. He does, it is true, reach the saddle "with about as much difficulty as he would have experienced in getting up the side of a first-rate man-of-war," but the silly animal persists in advancing "sideways," and, to add to his troubles, its rider is bidden to pick up the whip which Mr. Pickwick *would* drop at the least convenient moment. He manages to dismount without injury, but that finishes his equestrian feats, for the horse has its own methods of dealing with "sportsmen," and is soon going its own way, by itself.

It is a sorry exhibition, I am afraid, but there is worse to come at Dingley Dell. True, Mr. Winkle is "in a state of great honour and glory" while allowed to regale the company with the latest London stories, but the rook-shooting which Mr. Wardle proposes, only leads to further disasters. Mr. Pickwick and his non-sporting friends may cower "involuntarily to escape damage from the heavy fall of rooks," but their precautions are not really necessary. Mr. Winkle's gun seems at first inclined to mutiny. There is no more than a faint click when, so to speak, he brings it into action. But he has forgotten the cap. This fault is remedied, and Mr. Tupman is shot in the left arm. No wonder Mr. Pickwick's confidence is shaken, though things might have been considerably worse. It is to be noted, however, that Mr. Winkle himself is already profiting by his mistakes, for when the hour for the great cricket match grows near, he admits, without shame, that he is no cricketer.

Well, he is certainly wise, though some of us may regret that we are denied a glimpse of him—a short glimpse, it would have been—at the wicket.

Yet his trials and tribulations are by no means over. I need not speak of his brief friendship with Mrs. Pott of Eatanswill—the little indiscretion may be readily forgiven—but his second (and last) appearance with a gun must not be omitted. Mr. Winkle is no happier with this dangerous weapon when partridges are to be his victims than he was when the rooks failed to fall heavily, and you are not astonished to hear that the tall gamekeeper looks with some surprise at this peculiar guest who is holding his gun "as if he wished his coat-pocket to save him the trouble of pulling the trigger." Things, indeed, become so alarming as Mr. Winkle gets himself "mysteriously entangled with his gun" that the gamekeeper admonishes him with some severity. The poor man does his best, but still seems so set on committing manslaughter that Mr. Pickwick rightly refuses to move further in his wheelbarrow unless his young friend carries his gun with its muzzle to the ground.

Quite correctly and understandably Mr. Winkle objects: such a position would be "unsportsmanlike." Unfortunately he is less correct when he asks what the matter may be with the dogs' legs, as their owners point. It is a pity, too, that he permits his gun "to go off of its own account"—a property, by the way, that few guns possess—and it is almost too much when Tupman, of all people, brings down a bird. This, of course, is an accident, though old Wardle is not to know it, and Mr. Winkle is goaded into the most feverish activity. He

flashed, and blazed, and smoked away, without producing any material results worthy of being noted down; sometimes expending his charge in mid-air, and at others sending it skimming along so near the surface of the ground as to place the lives of the two dogs on a rather uncertain and precarious tenure. As a display of fancy shooting, it was extremely varied and curious; as an exhibition of firing with any precise object, it was, upon the whole, perhaps a failure. It is an established axiom that "every bullet has its billet." If it apply in an equal degree to shot, those of Mr. Winkle were unfortunate foundlings, deprived of their natural rights, cast loose upon the world, and billeted nowhere.

But at the end of it he promises to practise with a stuffed bird, and that, I feel, shows the right spirit.

Henceforth, except for his single appearance on skates,

we see Mr. Winkle in a more gracious rôle, and this is fully in keeping with the change in general construction which *Pickwick* by this time has undergone. Sport is thrust into the background and romance takes its place, beginning, appropriately enough, at the Christmas season. At old Wardle's house Mr. Winkle makes the acquaintance of Miss Arabella Allen, the "black-eyed young lady, in a very nice little pair of boots, with fur round the top," and his ambitions straightway undergo a very marked change. When the company is about to dance, the young couple cannot at once be found. Mr. Pickwick is annoyed. "What an extraordinary thing it is, Winkle," says he, "that you couldn't have taken your place before." "Not at all extraordinary," replies Mr. Winkle, and one's heart goes out to him, as, indeed, it also does to Mr. Pickwick, when a closer examination of the young lady brings to his lips that engagingly Pickwickian remark: "Well, I don't think that it *was* extraordinary, either, after all."

It may be assumed that the kiss which Mr. Winkle has bestowed on his Arabella has heartened him for the last of his sporting activities. His prowess on the ice is taken for granted, and neither want of practice nor the lack of skates is taken as an excuse. There is no way out, and we fear the worst. It duly comes.

"Now, then, sir," said Sam, in an encouraging tone; "off with you, and show 'em how to do it."

"Stop, Sam, stop!" said Mr. Winkle, trembling violently, and clutching hold of Sam's arms with the grasp of a drowning man. "How slippery it is, Sam!"

"Not an uncommon thing upon ice, sir," replied Mr. Weller. "Hold up, sir!"

This last observation of Mr. Weller's bore reference to a demonstration Mr. Winkle made, at the instant, of a frantic desire to throw his feet in the air and dash the back of his head on the ice.

"These—these—are very awkward skates; ain't they, Sam?" inquired Mr. Winkle, staggering.

"I'm afeerd there's a orkard gen'l'm'n in 'em, sir," replied Sam.

"Now, Winkle," cried Mr. Pickwick, quite unconscious that there was anything the matter. "Come; the ladies are all anxiety."

"Yes, yes," replied Mr. Winkle, with a ghastly smile; "I'm coming."

"Just a-goin' to begin," said Sam, endeavouring to disengage himself. "Now, sir, start off!"

"Stop an instant, Sam," gasped Mr. Winkle, clinging most affectionately to Mr. Weller. "I find I've got a couple of coats at home that I don't want, Sam. You may have them, Sam."

"Thank'ee, sir," replied Mr. Weller.

"Never mind touching your hat, Sam," said Mr. Winkle, hastily; "you needn't take your hand away to do that. I meant to have given you five shillings this morning for a Christmas-box, Sam. I'll give it you this afternoon, Sam."

"You're wery good, sir," replied Mr. Weller.

"Just hold me at first, Sam; will you?" said Mr. Winkle. "There—that's right. I shall soon get in the way of it, Sam. Not too fast, Sam; not too fast."

Mr. Winkle, stooping forward with his body half doubled up, was being assisted over the ice by Mr. Weller, in a very singular and unswanlike manner, when Mr. Pickwick most innocently shouted from the opposite bank,—

"Sam!"

"Sir?" said Mr. Weller.

"Here. I want you."

"Let go, sir," said Sam. "Don't you hear the governor a-callin'? Let go, sir."

With a violent effort, Mr. Weller disengaged himself from the grasp of the agonised Pickwickian, and in so doing administered a considerable impetus to the unhappy Mr. Winkle. With an accuracy which no degree of dexterity or practice could have ensured, that unfortunate gentleman bore swiftly down into the centre of the reel, at the very moment when Mr. Bob Sawyer was performing a flourish of unparalleled beauty. Mr. Winkle struck wildly against him, and with a loud crash they both fell heavily down. Mr. Pickwick ran to the spot. Bob Sawyer had risen to his feet, but Mr. Winkle was far too wise to do anything of the kind in skates. He was seated on the ice, making spasmodic efforts to smile; but anguish was depicted on every lineament of his countenance.

"Are you hurt?" inquired Mr. Benjamin Allen, with great anxiety.

"Not much," said Mr. Winkle, rubbing his back very hard.

"I wish you'd let me bleed you," said Mr. Benjamin, with great eagerness.

"No, I thank you," replied Mr. Winkle, hurriedly.

"I really think you had better," said Allen.

"Thank you," replied Mr. Winkle, "I'd rather not."

"What do *you* think, Mr. Pickwick?" inquired Bob Sawyer.

Mr. Pickwick was excited and indignant. He beckoned to Mr. Weller and said, in a stern voice, "Take his skates off."

"No; but really I had scarcely begun," remonstrated Mr. Winkle.

"Take his skates off," repeated Mr. Pickwick, firmly.

The command was not to be resisted. Mr. Winkle allowed Sam to obey it in silence.

"Lift him up," said Mr. Pickwick. Sam assisted him to rise.

Mr. Pickwick retired a few paces apart from the bystanders, and beckoning his friend to approach, fixed a searching look upon him, and uttered, in a low but distinct and emphatic tone, these remarkable words,—

"You're a humbug, sir."

"A what?" said Mr. Winkle, starting.

"A humbug, sir. I will speak plainer, if you wish it. An impostor, sir."

With these words Mr. Pickwick turned slowly on his heel, and rejoined his friends.

It is a dreadful, but not undeserved, reprimand.

That, however, is all. Mr. Pickwick's displeasure is of no long duration, and soon enough he is going out of his way to help his young friend. Mr. Winkle, too, is no less eager to assist his mentor, though here, alas, the wish and the deed are not quite the same thing. Is it too much to say that the disastrous verdict in *Bardell* v. *Pickwick* is largely due to that unlucky admission of Mr. Winkle's during cross-examination? Of course he is in a state of nervous agitation at the time, and cannot, I suppose, be blamed, but need he have blurted out those damaging words about Mr. Pickwick's suspicious behaviour towards *another* female? Could he not have accepted the great man's reasonable explanation that anybody is liable accidentally to enter the wrong bedroom in a hotel? But the admission has been made, and Serjeant Buzfuz makes the most of it.

Perhaps it is only what Dickens's contemporaries liked to call poetic justice that Mr. Winkle himself should, so soon afterwards, seem to be behaving suspiciously with a female. You will recall the unhappy affair which disturbs Bath's most respectable crescent in the middle of the night. Mrs. Dowler is being brought home at an exceedingly late hour in a sedan-chair. Her waiting spouse has succumbed to sleep, and Mr. Winkle is roused by the noise in the street. He rushes out improperly clothed, is insulted by both the chairmen, loses his light, is locked out, and in his terror of being recognised, bolts *into* the chair, from which Mrs. Dowler has not yet emerged. Mr. Dowler appears, and threatens to cut the throat—from ear to ear—of the villain who is so obviously running away with his wife. There is nothing for it but another flight. Mr. Winkle tears round the crescent, hotly pursued. He does succeed in regaining his bed, unharmed, but with the first ray of morning, flees to Bristol. A second challenge to a duel is a little too much for him.

There follows that stern chase, when Sam is ordered to bring him back at all costs, and when his victim, inquiring his way to Clifton, finds himself in Bob Sawyer's surgery, and learns from Mr. Allen of his sister's supposed "prior attachment." Sam duly finds the runaway, but on learning that Miss Arabella is somewhere in the neighbourhood, nobly agrees to join in the search for her, and—who will dare to worry about the coincidence?—meets the pretty housemaid (from Mr. Nupkins's) who has previously roused his admiration. Miss Arabella is discovered next door, and then it only remains for Mr. Pickwick to provide himself with a dark lantern and play fairy-godfather to the young people over the garden wall.

And here, be it noted, Mr. Winkle, who began in such a minor rôle, is called on to play a very important part indeed, for it is entirely owing to him that Mr. Pickwick regains his freedom. How, in prison, can he intercede with the unfriendly Mr. Allen on his sister's behalf? How interview old Winkle on his son's? In prison this is clearly impossible: Mr. Pickwick must pay up the damages demanded by Messrs. Dodson and Fogg. This he does in the most gracious way, and all is well. Mr. Allen, it is true, crushes his spectacles beneath the heel of his boot, and old Winkle is not an easy gentleman to deal with, but, once he has set his mind on anything Mr. Pickwick has a way with him, and the time soon comes when there is no further bar to the ex-sportsman's wedding.

Moreover, although Mr. Pott, who, you remember, turns up at this time in a part of the country that is unfortunately buff, exclaims "Serve him right" on being told the news, the marriage is all that it should be, and the curtain rings down on the happy information that Mr.

Nathaniel Winkle "presented all the external appearance of a civilised Christian ever afterwards."

A little overdrawn, this portrait of Winkle? Some of the episodes in which he takes part a little too near to impossible farce? What if they are? Everybody has met at least one would-be sportsman in his time, and none of them is without the Winkle touch. Analyse him, if you like, in the modern meticulous way, and you will discover a stage-figure with all the customary theatrical exaggerations; look at him as one of the Pickwickians, and he exactly fits. Nor, indeed, does he "date." There will be Winkles with us for as long as men continue to lift a gun to their shoulder, ride a horse, fix blades to their boots, or indulge in games played with a ball. The pity is that so few of them are either really droll in themselves or good to meet. Nathaniel Winkle, M.P.C., is both, but he is also considerably more! He is a great sportsman, *in the Pickwickian sense of the word*: a very great sportsman indeed.

AUGUSTUS SNODGRASS

and

THE REV. MR STIGGINS

By G. W. Stonier

III

MR. SNODGRASS is the least conspicuous of Pickwick's bodyguard. Dickens does not even bother to describe him; but one imagines, attached to that frightening and horsy name, a meek aspect, gentle manners, and the sort of smile which encourages others while keeping its own reserve. One is continually meeting people with such names—Mr. Beastly, Miss Grunter, and the like—who after the first moment of apprehension dwindle into insignificance. An exaggerated niceness, golden silence—what else, after all, have they to play for? Contentment may be theirs; the final harmony will be lacking. There are, of course, persons who succeed in being as disagreeable as their names; others, like Dickens's Mr. Venus, who carry off the fantasy —but for most of us the possession of an awkward nomenclature would serve only as a warning. "This is what I must *not* be !" Mr. Snodgrass, if he had chosen, might have gone about whistling through broken teeth or chewing a straw and smelling of middens; but for some reason he did not. Besides he had been christened Augustus.

Like Tupman and Winkle, like Mr. Pickwick for that matter, he springs into the novel ready-made, youthfully middle-aged and without antecedents. We are not tempted to wonder where he has come from. Prudence, an amiable self-effacement punctuated by moments of romantic dash, a somewhat prim devotion to the picturesque, the ability of quietly getting one's own way—these are his characteristics. He is hardly a striking or an attractive figure.

42

Mr. Weller attacks the executive of Ipswich.

When we first see him, sitting on Pickwick's left at the Club meeting, he is described as "mysteriously" clad in a blue coat with dogskin collar; that is all, not a word about himself. Tupman at least is permitted a jowl and a belly, and a name which would put to flight any virgin who happened to have a knowledge of the English language; even Winkle, in shooting-jacket and gaiters, comes on with a whiff of gunpowder. But Snodgrass is left featureless. He represents—a concession, one can't help feeling—arts.

　ᵐ the beginning the reader scents a faint ambiguity. To which portion of that pantomime horse, the Corresponding Society of the Pickwick Club, led by its trainer into so many smoking-rooms and provincial parlours, should Snodgrass be assigned—the head or the tail? At times, second only to Pickwick, he carries an air of seniority; but then there are long stretches of dumbness, of retirement, in which more and more he falls behind. How "strong," for example, was that "poetic turn" to which Pickwick always referred in presenting him to a newcomer? His notebook was usually ready, it is true, when there were loquacious strangers about—but that was part of the Club's stock-in-trade, they were all "students of human nature." Occasionally a hand is lifted, in the spirit of poesy, towards the clouds; by his instigation a story or a ballad is extracted from one of their numerous chance acquaintances. He visits Rochester Castle and exclaims "Magnificent ruin!" He listens spellbound to Mrs. Leo Hunter's *Ode to an Expiring Frog*. He has an impassioned argument with the lady who "does" the verse for the *Eatanswill Gazette*. And during the round game at Dingley Dell, while hands are being squeezed and cards lost, he whispers, we are told, poetical sentiments in his partner's ear. That seems to be the extent of his poetic accomplishment. A reputation among his friends of being a "great poet" is apparently sustained by the slenderest of props, with not even a Valentine or a Christmas motto to show.

Yet the odd thing about Mr. Snodgrass is not so much that he was a fraud—all the Pickwickians were that—but that, being a fraud, he should have escaped detection. While the others were busy enjoying themselves and making fools of themselves abroad, skating and shooting, driving, archæologising, fighting duels or getting entangled in breach-of-promise cases, he alone kept clear of misfortunes; until the reader begins to suspect in him the protective cunning of such defenceless creatures as the tapir. Look up that fateful chapter in which a gamekeeper is nearly killed and Pickwick is discovered drunk in a wheelbarrow and taken to the stocks—"Mr. Snodgrass had preferred to stay at home." Wily, cosy Mr. Snodgrass ! It cannot always be by accident. Moreover, he was the sort of friend who offers assistance at the wrong moment and in the wrong direction.

"The Doctor, I believe, is a very good shot," said Mr. Winkle.

"Most of these military men are," observed Mr. Snodgrass calmly; "but so are you, an't you?"

Mr. Winkle replied in the affirmative; and perceiving that he had not alarmed his companion sufficiently, changed his ground.

"Snodgrass," he said, in a voice tremulous with emotion, "if I fall, you will find in a packet which I shall place in your hands a note for my—for my father."

This attack was a failure also. Mr. Snodgrass was affected, but he undertook the delivery of the note as readily as if he had been a Twopenny Postman.

"If I fall," said Mr. Winkle, "or if the Doctor falls, you, my dear friend, will be tried as an accessory before the fact. Shall I involve my friend in transportation—possibly for life!"

Mr. Snodgrass winced a little at this, but his heroism was invincible. "In the cause of friendship," he fervently exclaimed, "I will brave all dangers."

How Mr. Winkle cursed his friend's devoted friendship internally, as they walked silently along, side by side, for some minutes, each immersed in his own meditations! The morning was wearing away; he grew desperate.

"Snodgrass," he said, stopping suddenly, "do *not* let me be baulked in this matter—do *not* give information to the local authorities—do *not* obtain the assistance of several peace officers, to take either me or Doctor Slammer, of the Ninety-seventh Regiment, at present quartered in Chatham Barracks, into custody, and thus prevent the duel—I say, do *not*."

Mr. Snodgrass seized his friend's hand warmly, as he enthusiastically replied, "Not for worlds!"

There, you can interpret him yourself. Towards Winkle his behaviour is persistently merciless. Not only did he push Winkle forward as far as he could in the affair with Dr. Slammer, plying him afterwards with liquor and weapons and an abundance of powder, but when his unlucky friend had to go skating—a misfortune hardly less disastrous—it was Snodgrass, "knowing as little about the matter as a Hindoo," who helped to buckle on the skates.

We await his own downfall with a slightly malicious glee. The invitation to Mrs. Leo Hunter's breakfast seems propitious. In advance he swallows her ridiculous poem—good. He will go as a Troubadour. The morning comes. Dressed in blue satin trunks and cloak, white silk tights and shoes, and wearing on top of all a Grecian helmet, he sets out for that "Eastern fairy-land" of the county Muse.

The grounds were more than an acre and a quarter in extent, and they were filled with people! Never was such a blaze of beauty, and fashion, and literature. There was the young lady who "did" the poetry in the Eatanswill Gazette, in the garb of a sultana, leaning upon the arm of the young gentleman who "did" the review department, and who was appropriately habited in a field marshal's uniform. . . . There were hosts of these geniuses, and any reasonable person would have thought it honour enough to meet them. But more than these, there were half a dozen lions from London—authors, real authors, who had written whole books, and printed them afterwards—and here you might see 'em walking about, like ordinary men, smiling and talking. . . . And above all, there was Mrs. Leo Hunter, in the character of Minerva, receiving the company. . . .

"Ah," you think, "now for Snodgrass's collapse. Till now he's been lucky. In front of them all he'll be challenged to write a sonnet or asked to recite. One of the London authors will pop him a question about Hood. And then Pickwick will jump up and call him a humbug. *Something*, at any rate, is going to happen." But nothing does. Snodgrass comes through with flying colours.

From that point, I think, our attitude to Snodgrass undergoes a change. In a mild way he is invincible; he never even loses his temper. The sneaking regard we have felt all along for this poky, receding, stiff-necked, dimly attitudinising man becomes almost affection. Wise little Snodgrass! There must have been times when the society of his fellow Pickwickians became unendurable, when any sensitive man would have run miles to escape their corporate geniality. Those sessions in the "commercial room" at night, among hard-drinking voluble eccentrics and dingy bores, to be followed next morning by the resurrection of Pickwick over a ham and a frothing tankard—no wonder Mr. Snodgrass had his fits of melancholy when he held his tongue and preferred to stay at home; with an eye, no doubt, on the local Heppel. He sometimes missed his round: I remember at least one occasion when he pretended an extraordinary interest in somebody he was talking to and so avoided having his glass filled. Excess, of any sort, was as disagreeable to him as needless physical exercise. He was not a good mixer, and no one could have regulated his enthusiasms more exactly. The only exception to this was during an evening at the Peacock, when a dirty-faced individual with a clay pipe had announced, "Rum creeturs is women," and Snodgrass, enlivened perhaps by gin, or having taken stock of the company, came out with an affirmation. "Women, after all," he said, "are the great props and comforts of our existence. . . ." (It is his only recorded apophthegm.) ". . . Show me the man who says anything against women, as women, and I boldly declare he is not a man." His fist made the glasses ring. But even this indiscretion had its reason, its Snodgrassian justification: he already had an eye on Emily Wardle, and a comfortable marriage was preparing in the future.

Much of his smugness and snugness we can forgive and even regard with affection. In the reflected light of extravagant adventures he holds back a little, rigid, formulating a gesture, abashed and yet confident, wanting if he can to help, but secretly glad to be out of it. There is no doubt that he was attracted by *other* people's high jinks, that he warmed himself at the bonfire. He starts a conversation and then drops out, or interposes a remark when the others have fallen silent; he is always ready to take the rear seat on the coach, to intervene in a tiff, to haul back Mr. Pickwick by the tails. Our pleasure in some of the liveliest scenes, when voices are raised and heels flying, is increased by the knowledge that Snodgrass, also, is there. And in the first place it was very clever of him to have worked his way into the Club at all, aloof as he was from the usual Pickwickian accomplishments. Mr. Pickwick knew rather less about poetry than Mr. Snodgrass did about skates; "my poetic friend Snodgrass" added a graceful, an unexpected feather to his cap.

It cannot be said that he overwhelmed them with poetry. Blake's death in August, 1827, when they were following the Eatanswill election, was allowed to pass unnoticed. There is no record of Snodgrass quoting Shakespeare, Chaucer, Keats, Milton, or any other great poet; or indeed of his having heard of any of them. How Mr. Pickwick would have taken a quotation from Shakespeare, unless it had come out of a birthday book, I do not know; but it would probably have frightened him. No, Snodgrass knew better; he had discovered, far below the masters, a poetic world in which it was possible for an ordinary mortal to stroll. There, a bountiful Nature is always triumphant, the sun rises gladly and sets sadly, the birds sing, flowers gaily blow in meadows sentinelled by silent trees, mountains surge majestically, a stream winds its way murmuring to the ocean which is a symbol of our lives. The inhabitants of this land, whom we see through an old archway or framed by trees and clouds, are poets and lovers, kings, princesses, women singing softly to their babes, old men who wander over the countryside. Love is either eternal or fickle as the moon. There is anger in the tempest, pathos in the rose which hides a thorn. Our moods and sentiments are echoed by the places in which we find ourselves; and thus there are whole landscapes of jocundity, grief, childhood, expectation, connubial bliss. When we frown the sun disappears and our path leads through a gloomy wood; we think of music and Nature becomes symphonic, with larks, cowbells, and waterfalls. Happy land, where all is complaisance, where the soul and its surroundings are one!

How Mr. Snodgrass first came upon it, whether in youthful daydreams or turning the pages of a *Keepsake* on Sunday afternoons, we are not told; but he had made it his own. What a comfort to escape the acerbities of daily life and possess a realm in which fancy was realised at every turn! The flowers in the garden became his thoughts, the clouds brought messages of hope. One morning his heart would be a spring bubbling in distant woods; the next, a shipwreck or a tomb, or

> a violet robbed of breath
> By the strong whirlwind in an hour of gloom.

Rochester Castle, in the company of Winkle, might have been well enough, but there were other Castles—Otranto, Ormonde, Drachenfels. He could travel, too, where he liked, exchanging Bath for Venice, Ipswich for Constantinople, the stage-coach for a gondola or a barge. His Grecian helmet at Mrs. Leo Hunter's was nothing; in solitude he was accustomed to togas, caps with ostrich plumes, the uniform of a crusader.

> I'll hang my harp on the willow tree,
> And I'll go to the war again,
> For a peaceful home has no charm for me,
> A battlefield no pain.

And—possibly the greatest discovery of all—MELANCHOLY has its balm. Snodgrass's life was not unhappy, and those periods in it when he refuses to do or say anything, and seems to be sulking, were probably filled with moments of acute pleasure. How agreeable it must have been, during the long speeches of the Pickwick trial or while the cricket match was in progress, to let one's imagination roam over deserted shores, landscapes with ruined towers, a faded bunch of letters, the solitary Nemesis of the poet—

> Deep embowered from mortal ken
> Thread we now a Poet's Den!
> Bright confusion reveals there,
> Ne'er had she a realm more fair!
> 'Tis a wilderness of mind
> Redolent of tastes refined. . . .
> By the open lattice sitting,
> Fevered dreams of beauty flitting
> O'er his heart and o'er his brain
> In one bright unbroken chain;
> Drinking deep through every sense
> Draughts of pleasure, too intense,—
> Mark the poet's glistening eye
> Wandering now o'er earth and sky!

Yes, there were consolations. Even a broken heart—and Snodgrass, if only as a poet, must have had his experiences —could be turned to beauty. Perhaps it was as the result of such an affair that he joined the Pickwick Club.

> Oh, no, we never mention her,
>   Her name is never heard,
> My lips are now forbid to speak
>   That once familiar word;
> From sport to sport they hurry me
>   To banish my regret
> And when they win a smile from me
>   They fancy I forget.

In a matter of this kind the Pickwickians would have shown delightful tact—and one knows, as I have pointed out already, that for some reason they let him down lightly. Had the break been his fault or hers?

> She never blamed him—never,
>> But received him when he came
> With a welcome sort of shiver,
>> And she tried to look the same.

If the affair existed, we may be sure that Snodgrass—oh, quite innocently—made the most of it. The titles of some of his poems suggest themselves: "Love's Wealth," "Lines on a portrait of a Shepherdess," "The Forsaken," "My Own Fireside." And we may be sure that he made a quick recovery, reserving his sorrow, afterwards, for special occasions.

Nevertheless my general view of him as a poet is that he tended to buoyant sentiment. The Della Cruscans (rather before his time) and "snivelling" Jerningham might have attracted him as strange exotics, but he would not have followed them. He would have preferred, I think, to be known as "the English Anacreon."

> I'd be a butterfly born in a bower
> Kissing all buds that are pretty and sweet.

Haynes Bayly, Lord Morpeth, the Hon. Charles Phipps, Alaric M. Watts, Archdeacon Spencer—these were probably the poets to whom he turned most often. He had discovered the advantage of poetastry over poetry: that it is accessible, and rewards the reader with familiar delights. Moreover, it encourages humdrum natures to detect their particular flutter. I do not think that Mr. Snodgrass was altogether humdrum, but his inclination was lazy and domestic.

> I'd be a butterfly, sportive and airy,
> Rocked in a rose when the nightingale sings.

How relieved he must have been when the romantic gesture of an elopement with Emily became unnecessary, and he could settle down in the country to years of torpid ease. No more paper-chases with Pickwick, no more pretending with Winkle or reassuring Tupman! Earlier in the story, during the first visit to the Wardles, we have been given a foretaste of pleasures to come. Snodgrass stands with his back to the fire sipping a cherry-brandy before supper and glancing round with "heart-felt satisfaction." The room was large—

with a red-brick floor and a capacious chimney; the ceiling garnished with hams, sides of bacon, and ropes of onions. The walls were decorated with several hunting whips, two or three bridles, and an old rusty blunderbuss, with an inscription below it, intimating that it was "Loaded"—as it had been, on the same authority, for half a century at least. An old eight-day clock, of solemn and sedate demeanour, ticked gravely in one corner; and a silver watch, of equal antiquity, dangled from one of the many hooks which ornamented the dresser.

The picture of a farm of his own in Dingley Dell had already formed. He saw his way. Our last glimpse of him, happily married and comfortably settled, is the most touching; nothing disturbs his peace.

> I'd be a butterfly, living a rover,
> Dying when fair things are far away.

THE REV. MR STIGGINS

VERY often the minor characters of Dickens are the best, and a reader who had forgotten many things about *Pickwick*, for whom Snodgrass was a name and a profile on a cigarette card, might retain a vivid memory of Stiggins. He is revealed by one of those tortuous approaches, like a London street, which are the charm of Dickens narratives; Mr. Pickwick engages Sam Weller as his man-servant, Sam pays a visit to his father, and there, in the old gentleman's absence, ensconced by the fire in rusty black among pineapple rums and buttered toast, sits the Rev. Mr. Stiggins. We catch that rattlesnake eye at once—the face suggestive of a starchier Widow Twankey, a close-buttoned waistcoat, trousers hitched high over black cotton stockings; it is like turning up one of those odd familiar figures in Snap. The wide-brimmed hat, worn beaver gloves, and derelict umbrella by his side suggest a flying visit, but we know that he will stop for hours. He has his nose to think of— not a tragic nose like Cyrano's, nor a truant nose like Major Kovalyov's, nor a beacon like Pistol's—but a thin, gristly nose, attractive to north-easters, which must be pigmented with sips of tea and nips of rum: delightful combination, appropriate both to the gossip and the boozer in his temperament. Without this comfort his groans would have a less hollow roll, his piety less unction.

Yet there is nothing sinister about Mr. Stiggins, as there is about so many minor Tartuffes. His black wrappings do not horrify us by being coupled, say, with the arts of seduction. He wants such simple things—food, drink, money, the companionship of admiring "sisters"—he goes about getting them in such a simple way; and we accept him in the Weller household like some objectionable pet monkey with which amiable people will sometimes startle their friends. Sooner or later, we know, old Mr. Weller will lay hands on him and he will never return.

He is creepy only in the stage sense of the word. How admirably he makes his entrance to that final scene, when he has come to ask if Mrs. Weller has left him her money! A tap at the door is followed by another, then a whole row of taps; after a pause, the door slowly opens, a red face with long black locks appears, hesitates; finally the whole body is squeezed through, and Mr. Stiggins glides into the room, closing the door gently behind him. That is in the stage convention (remember the stammerer in *The Bartered Bride*), but how deliciously, how freshly Dickens has put this piece of acting into words! Dickens is often accused as a novelist of exaggeration, and Stiggins, like all purely comic figures, is of course exaggerated, but he is never overdone. We do not have too much of him. He is a shining example of Dickens's restraint in caricature.

MR TUPMAN
By J. W. T. Ley

IV

A CONTEMPORARY reviewer of *The Pickwick Papers* asserted that Winkle, Snodgrass, and Tupman were very uninteresting personages, having peculiarities rather than characters; that they were "useless incumbrances which the author seems to have admitted hastily among his *dramatis personæ* without well knowing what to do with them." Useless incumbrances! Winkle on the ice! The shooting party! The arbour scene at Dingley Dell! The world agrees that young Boz made amazingly good use of those "incumbrances." The assumption that the author admitted these three characters to the book without well knowing what to do with them was correct, of course, but that he did do something very effective with them is undeniable.

Tupman, Winkle, and Snodgrass are not insignificant bodies in the *Pickwick* firmament shining merely by the reflected light of its brilliant sun. They are lesser suns whose light is dimmed by contact with that of the greater orb.

It would appear beyond doubt that when he wrote the first chapter young Boz had greater hopes of Tupman than of either of the others. To the introduction of Snodgrass and Winkle he devoted one sentence. Of Tupman we have a quite detailed description:

"On his right hand sat Mr. Tracy Tupman—the too susceptible Tupman, who to the wisdom and experience of maturer years superadded the enthusiasm and ardour of a boy, in the most interesting and pardonable of human weaknesses—love. Time

The fat boy awake, on this occasion only.

and feeling had expanded that once romantic form; the black silk waistcoat had become more and more developed; inch by inch had the gold watch-chain beneath it disappeared from within the range of Tupman's vision; and gradually had the capacious chin encroached upon the borders of the white cravat; but the soul of Tupman had known no change—admiration of the fair sex was still its ruling passion."

To those who know their Dickens that introduction definitely suggests that he had real hopes of Tupman.

One noteworthy feature of this book is the little we know about the four characters in whom our interest is consistently maintained. Not until very late do we learn that Mr. Winkle had been permitted to see a little of the world prior to entering his father's business in Birmingham. Of Mr. Pickwick himself we learn in the most casual way that he had made a modest competency in business and retired. Of Messrs. Tupman and Snodgrass we know really nothing—a fact which, like Mr. Weller's philosophical remark about death and undertakers, opens up a wide field for speculation.

It would appear that Pickwick and Tupman were friends of some years' standing. The leader would seem to have been the younger of the two. Mr. Pickwick was— is—round about fifty years of age, rather under than over. When it was suggested that he should go on the slide at Dingley Dell, he protested that he had not done such a thing "these thirty years," remarking also that he used to slide in the gutters when he was a boy. The opening description of Mr. Tupman surely suggests that he was older than that? There is further evidence in the scene which occurred prior to the *fête champêtre* at Mrs. Leo Hunter's:

"I shall go as a Bandit," interrupted Mr. Tupman.

"What!" said Mr. Pickwick with a sudden start.

"As a bandit," repeated Mr. Tupman mildly.

"You don't mean to say," said Mr. Pickwick gazing with solemn firmness at his friend. "You don't mean to say, Mr. Tupman, that it is your intention to put yourself into a green velvet jacket with a two-inch tail?"

"Such *is* my intention, sir," replied Mr. Tupman warmly. "And why not, sir!"

"Because, sir," said Mr. Pickwick considerably excited, "because you are too old, sir."

"Too old!" exclaimed Mr. Tupman.

"And if any further ground of objection be wanting," continued Mr. Pickwick, "you are too fat, sir."

"Sir," said Mr. Tupman, his face suffused with a crimson glow. "This is an insult."

"Sir," replied Mr. Pickwick in the same tone. "It is not half the insult to you that your appearance in my presence in a green velvet jacket with a two-inch tail would be to me."

Then ensued the most painful scene in the book. Mr. Pickwick reiterated his assertion that his friend was both old and fat. Messrs. Winkle and Snodgrass looked on, petrified at beholding such a scene between two such men. Physical violence was averted by the intervention of Snodgrass, and the two old friends revealed a magnanimity worthy of them, but it would seem a reasonable deduction that Mr. Pickwick's statements were true—that it was his consciousness of their truth that caused Mr. Tupman so hotly to resent them.

What then was his purpose in becoming one of the Travelling Members of the Pickwick Club? There is nothing known of him to support any suggestion that he was merely a lascivious old man bent on an ogling expedition. Only once is there any record of a lapse into impropriety, and even in that case the suggestion may be put forward presently that he has suffered injustice through a rather careless slip by the Editor of the Club's Transactions. He was too susceptible, but that is a failing, not a vice, and goodness knows he suffered for it!

The truth, I think, is that Mr. Datchery's description of himself as "merely a single buffer getting through life upon his means as idly as he could," may fairly be applied to Tupman. Pickwick himself, in setting out upon his peregrinations, was inspired by lofty motives—the desire to benefit the human race; Winkle and Snodgrass were young men "finishing" their educations. As to Tupman, we can only theorise. Let it be suggested then, that he, like his revered leader, had retired from business on a modest competency, and that he had found the loneliness of his bachelor life unendurable. For who can doubt but that in his bachelor chambers, his heart often beat sorely under his capacious waistcoat when memories of many might-have-beens crowded his mind? To such a man, still susceptible, as Tupman was, the reflection that "'Tis better to have loved and lost than never to have loved at all," can bring but little comfort. What more natural than, that he should readily seize the opportunity of seeking nepenthes amid the distractions of new scenes, new experiences, new acquaintances, in the company of his old friend in business, Mr. Pickwick?

There is much to suggest that Dickens had a greater regard for Tupman than for either of the other followers of Mr. Pickwick. He is the central figure in many of the best depicted incidents in the book, and only on one occasion can it be said that he wholly lacks dignity. That, of course, is the occasion already alluded to, when he insisted on appearing at Mrs. Hunter's rout as a bandit in a green jacket with a two-inch tail. It is an age-old saying that there is no fool like an old fool, and a too susceptible old buck is bound to possess in considerable degree the quality of absurdity, but while this applies to Tupman, it is also true—is it not?—that throughout the book—even in his moment of most cruel humiliation—he retains a certain dignity which compels a measure of respect and wins our sympathy. After all, the letter that he addressed to Mr. Pickwick, after his betrayal by Jingle and the spinster aunt, has a certain dignity about it: while expressive of—shall we say?—both humiliation and heart-break, it is commendably free from self-pity. It breathes the spirit of comedy, of course, but it does not wholly lack an element of dignity. We sense, in fact, an underlying sympathy on the part of the author with the humiliated Tupman. May the explanation lie in the fact that Tupman's creator had himself not long before suffered the pangs and humiliation of unrequited love? In his newly-married bliss, young Boz found himself able to smile at love-lorn swains, but his own experience was yet too recent for him to be able entirely to withhold sympathy.

Moreover, there is generally a definite suggestion of staidness about Tupman. He is never guilty of the venial lapses which are recorded of the other three Pickwickians. What might have happened if he had accompanied them to the dinner which followed the All Muggleton *v.* Dingley Dell cricket match were a fruitless speculation; suffice it that there is no instance on record of his having fallen a victim either to wine or to salmon. For example, in the evening of the ball at Rochester he was the only one of the four who remained sober. "The wine, which had exerted its somniferous influence over Mr. Snodgrass and Mr. Winkle, had stolen upon the senses of Mr. Pickwick," but Tupman was sober, and actually the stimulus of a glass of wine was necessary to induce him to screw up his determination to attend the ball.

For the contretemps that ensued, Winkle had only himself to blame. His condition of alcoholic coma was such that his consent could not be sought to the loan of his coat to the volatile stranger, and to that fact he owed his nerve-racking experience of the following morning. It may be argued that Tupman was presuming somewhat in abstracting the coat and lending it to Jingle, but Winkle was neither capable of attending the ball nor of giving permission for the loan, and while Tupman himself would have been glad to lend a change of apparel, Jingle was rather slim and he himself was—"rather fat—grown-up Bacchus." There in that ballroom at the Bull would be bevies of lovely Kentish women, but amorous bachelors of his age are apt to suffer acutely from shyness, from diffidence, from self-consciousness. His friends could not accompany him; he could not screw up his courage to go alone; the very attractive stranger could not attend without suitable attire, and there was none but Winkle's available. It would surely be unjust to criticise Tupman for what he did in such circumstances.

We have referred to his shyness, his self-consciousness; does it not appear that Tupman knew better what it was to be in love with love than to be in love? How else shall we understand his astonishment at the arts by which Jingle cut out Dr. Slammer? He had his dance with Mrs. Budger, thanks entirely to his more enterprising companion, but even his demeanour in the dance was such as to suggest that he would have had a poor time of it if he had gone to the ball alone. He hopped about we are told, "with a face expressive of the most intense solemnity, dancing (as a good many people do) as if a quadrille were not a thing to be laughed at, but a severe trial to the feelings, which it requires inflexible resolution to encounter." Can we wonder that he had suffered many disappointments in love!

But Jingle's example had its influence. It seems to have awakened him to a realisation of the fact that he who hesitates has precious little chance with the fair sex. Henceforth we observe in him no more of that restraining diffidence which characterised him at the ball. There was a review at Chatham the next day but one, and the Pickwickians attended. Very early on Tupman mysteriously disappeared, to be discovered some time later by Mr. Pickwick—exhausted by the pursuit of his own hat—seated on the top of a barouche, supremely happy, sublimely free from self-consciousness, in the company of the two Wardle girls and their spinster aunt. There he was, "as easy and unconcerned as if he had belonged to the family from the first moment of his infancy." The explanation of his presence in this company was a perfectly reasonable one, but his complete at-homeness surprises us after having seen him at the ball. He has acquired a new confidence. Just listen:

"Young ladies have *such* spirits," said Miss Wardle, with an air of gentle commiseration, as if animal spirits were contraband and their possession without a permit, a high crime and misdemeanour.

"Oh, they have," replied Mr. Tupman, not exactly making the sort of reply that was expected from him. "It's quite delightful."

"Hem!" said Miss Wardle, rather dubiously.

"Will you permit me," said Mr. Tupman in his blandest manner, touching the enchanting Rachel's wrist with one hand and gently elevating the bottle with the other. "Will you permit me?"

"Oh, sir!" Mr. Tupman looked most impressive and Rachel expressed her fear that more guns were going off, in which case, of course, she would have required support again.

"Do you think my dear nieces pretty?" whispered their affectionate aunt to Mr. Tupman.

"I should, *if* their aunt wasn't there," replied the ready Pickwickian, with a passionate glance.

Truly a very different Tupman from him who had danced with Mrs. Budger two nights previously!

All this was the prelude to one of the most memorable love dramas ever recorded by an English novelist. The next day, the Pickwickians proceeded to Dingley Dell, and for a time the course of true love must have seemed to Mr. Tupman to be a railroad, both from the point of view of smoothness and from that of speed. But here notice must be taken of an incident which, if it be correctly recorded, must always be regretted by admirers of this amiable man. After Mr. Winkle's hopeless attempt to ride and Mr. Pickwick's failure to drive, the four friends arrived at their destination on foot, with "torn clothes, lacerated faces, dusty shoes, exhausted looks, and above all, the horse." They were heartily welcomed none the less, and after being washed, mended, brushed, and brandied they "traversed several dark passages, and being joined by Mr. Tupman, who had lingered behind to snatch a kiss from Emma, for which he had been duly rewarded with sundry kickings and scratchings, arrived at the parlour door."

Can this be true of the Tupman who had made such progress with Emily's aunt the previous day? If it be, we have no option but to agree with the late Percy Fitzgerald that such conduct was "an extraordinary proceeding on the part of a stout, elderly gentleman who was a new guest and had barely entered the house." But dare it be suggested that the young Editor of the Transactions of the Pickwick Club was here guilty of a lapse—that he wrote Tupman for Snodgrass? Such conduct on Tupman's part would be reprehensible in the light of what had gone before and of what we know was to proceed forthwith, whereas it would have been perfectly natural on Snodgrass's part, for be it remembered that on the previous day he had progressed quite as satisfactorily with Emily as had Tupman with the spinster aunt. It is the only suggestion in the book of conduct on our friend's part that can be described as in bad taste, and the suggestion that the lapse was the Editor's and not his will no doubt be acceptable to his admirers.

Three love affairs progressed rapidly that evening: Isabella Wardle and Mr. Trundle "went partners" and Emily Wardle and Mr. Snodgrass did the same, "and even Mr. Tupman and the spinster aunt established a joint-stock company of fish and flattery," and "when the spinster aunt got 'matrimony' the young ladies laughed afresh and the spinster aunt seemed disposed to be pettish till, feeling Mr. Tupman squeezing her hand under the table, *she* brightened up too, and looked rather knowing, as if matrimony in reality were not quite so far off as some people thought." That he had indeed made good progress was revealed the next morning when Mr. Winkle, instead of shooting at the pigeon and wounding the crow, shot at the crow and wounded the pigeon; when, in other words, Mr. Tupman saved the lives of innumerable birds by receiving the discharge from his friend's gun in his left arm. His wounds bound up, the party returned to the house.

"What's the matter?" screamed the ladies.
"Mr. Tupman has met with a little accident; that's all."
The spinster aunt uttered a piercing scream, burst into an hysteric laugh and fell backwards into the arms of her nieces.

She loved him! Thus through pain and tribulation did he find joy. But, as all the world knows, the course of true love was not to maintain smoothness for very long. The happy couple were to snatch just a few hours of bliss and then dreams were to be shattered for both. No need to recall it all in detail. The Fat Boy woke up for a few brief moments, the unscrupulous Jingle appeared on the scene, and the courses of two lives were altered. There was no hope for Tupman where Jingle was. Nothing can excuse the spinster aunt, but it is clear that this adventurer had "a way with him," for before he had been at Dingley Dell an hour, nieces, as well as aunt, were his fascinated admirers. On the other hand, Tupman's conduct is not open to criticism. There was no impropriety in an elderly bachelor of means seeking the hand of a semi-elderly spinster, and that he was so easily fooled by Jingle is evidence of the simplicity of his unsuspecting nature.

How long Mr. Tupman remained in seclusion at Cobham—"for a misanthrope's choice one of the prettiest and most desirable places of residence I ever met with"—we do not know. We next meet him with the others at Mr. Pickwick's lodgings in Goswell Street, but what length of time had elapsed we are not told. We can only guess what his feelings may have been when he found his leader in that compromising situation with Mrs. Bardell. There is, indeed, but little need to follow his subsequent movements. He was later, of course, to have the satisfaction of witnessing the final exposure of Jingle. Knowing him as we do, as the possessor of very human qualities, we cannot but suspect that the trembling of his voice when he read aloud, at Mr. Pickwick's request, the letter from Messrs. Dodson and Fogg, was due in part, at least, to just a touch of maliciousness! Only a moment before, Mr. Pickwick had been remarking "that we seem destined to enter no man's house without involving him in some degree of trouble. Does it not, I ask, bespeak the indiscretion, or, worse than that, the blackness of heart—that I should say so!—of my followers that, beneath whatever roof they locate, they disturb the peace of mind and happiness of some confiding female?" That was an utterly unjust charge so far as Tupman was concerned, and if he experienced just a touch of unholy joy when, a moment later, it fell to his lot to read the letter notifying his leader of Mrs. Bardell's action, he may surely be forgiven.

Be it noted that Tupman, so far as we know—and we certainly do know that he never married—avoided for the remainder of his life entanglements with members of the fair sex. He had learned his lesson, and it is worthy of remark that at the Christmas party at Dingley Dell, while we are expressly told that Pickwick kissed the old lady, and Winkle kissed Arabella, and Snodgrass kissed Emily, and Mr. Weller kissed all the female servants, and the poor relations kissed everybody, there is no mention of Tupman thus indulging. Indeed, his only appearance in the account of that party is at the beginning, when, probably with memories of the scene prior to Mrs. Leo Hunter's rout, he presumed to comment on the fact that Mr. Pickwick had doffed his gaiters and appeared in speckled silk stockings!

Mr. Tupman was not a sportsman and, to his credit, he made no professions in that direction. It is indeed true to say that he never pretended to be anything that he was not. That cannot be said of Winkle; nor, we suspect, can it be said of Snodgrass, for the only evidence we have of his being a poet is his pose. He did not attempt either to skate or to slide, but when Mr. Pickwick fell through the ice he did *do* something. By way of "rendering the promptest assistance, and at the same time conveying to any persons who might be within hearing the clearest possible notion of the catastrophe" he ran off across country at his utmost speed, screaming "Fire!" with all his might. It may not have been a very effective something, but it *was* calculated to raise an alarm, and in any case it betokened more initiative than Snodgrass's, "Keep yourself up for an instant—for only an instant!" or Winkle's, "Yes, do; let me implore you—for my sake!"

It is true that he did join a shooting expedition on one occasion, but he made no pretence at expertness with the gun, and we are expressly told that his mode of proceeding evinced far more of prudence and deliberation than that adopted by Mr. Winkle. He realised that the two great points to be attained were, first to discharge his piece without injury to himself, and secondly to do so without danger to the bystanders, and so he shut his eyes firmly and fired into the air. If only Winkle had exercised such prudence on a former occasion!

There remains to be noted one aspect of Mr. Tupman's character which his admirers would fain avoid, but even the greatest of men is still a little lower than the angels. No man, though he be Mr. Pickwick himself, is free from some human failing, and so it were not only futile but foolish to attempt to hide or ignore the fact that Mr. Tupman lacked that spirit of benevolence which characterised his great leader. Regret it though we may—as we do—we cannot escape it. Mr. Tupman's heart did not throb in sympathy with those of his fellow men who had suffered worldly misfortune. The number of instances recorded on the Transactions of the Society, in which that excellent man referred objects of charity to the houses of other members for left-off garments or pecuniary relief is, we are told, "almost incredible." The truth is that poor Tupman was a little too self-centred to achieve true greatness. But disappointment in love has warped many a fine character. Tupman had suffered many times. To know all is to forgive all. Let not this one failing be allowed to weigh too heavily in the balance. It cannot be said of Tupman, as it was said of another immortal: "Sir, he was a great man, a very great man," but it can be said that he was a lovable man, a companionable man, for whose existence the world is a happier place. He has added to our permanent stock of harmless merriment; for that he merits our gratitude, is worthy of honour.

SAMUEL WELLER
By John Betjeman

V

I DON'T like Phiz's drawing of Sam Weller. It is the only figure in his illustrations to *Pickwick* that I don't like. I re-read *Pickwick* the other day in an edition not published by the esteemed publishers of this book and of the original Dickens. Though the illustrations in every other respect fell far short of the text—and normally I regard the original illustrations of all Dickens's novels as an indispensable concomitant—the depiction of Sam Weller seemed highly suitable. It showed a young man of neat figure and sharp features clad in the fashion of the late Georgian days. His face was not unhandsome. Indeed, he looked to me very like some rather amusing and clever fellow of the type which now supplies you with petrol at a garage and tells you something is wrong with the engine, thus bringing in a little extra profit to his employer. Sam Weller has always seemed to me a sharp, human and likely person, far more probable than any other character in the book.

Phiz shows you a rakish rather emaciated person, a sort of youthful Bill Sykes, or one of those harum-scarum characters in Lever. I think it is because his drawing is so much more caricature than exact portraiture that Phiz was never able to draw a satisfactory Sam Weller. For Sam Weller is one of the few characters in Dickens who is not caricature. Even Mr. Pickwick, who ends up such a lovable humanitarian, starts off as a stiff almost tedious pedant. As for Snodgrass, Winkle, and Tupman, they are less convincingly drawn by the writer than they are by the artist.

First appearance of M.ʳ Samuel Weller.

You will remember some of the last words of Sam Weller to Mr. Pickwick: "If you vant a more polished sort o' feller, vell and good, have him; but vages or no vages, notice or no notice, board or no board, lodgin' or no lodgin', Sam Veller, as you took from the old inn in the Borough, sticks by you come what may; and let ev'rythin' and ev'rybody do their wery fiercest, nothin' shall ever perwent it!"

Those words are consistent with the "bit of a wag" who was originally taken on in the Borough.

"You accept the situation?" inquired Mr. Pickwick.

"Cert'nly," replied Sam. "If the clothes fits me half as well as the place, they'll do."

As soon as Sam Weller appears he seems to put new life not only into the Pickwick Club, but also into their inventor. A series of jokes like that of Bill Stumps his mark. Too many madman's manuscripts, stories of Dying Clowns or Bagmen's stories interspersed with the rather elaborate humour of the proceedings of the Club would have made Mr. Pickwick little more than one of those illustrated comic periodicals which you may still pick up in a tattered and forgotten condition on the book-stalls of the Farringdon Road.

But Sam Weller draws out Dickens from the caricaturist into the realistic painter. He seems to give him leisure. There is no less of the liveliness but more of the beauty of Dickens's extraordinary and copious flow of unbelievably skilful prose. Just as Rowlandson seems to forget Syntax and display his genius for landscape and architectural illustration in the backgrounds to his aquatints of the Three Tours, so Dickens is inspired by his background to produce livelier and lovelier work.

Obviously at first Sam Weller was intended as occasional incident, but as the book proceeds the background comes forward and the foreground sinks back. At Dingley Dell Sam's powers of companionship and joviality are more marked. You will remember how he led the servants in their cheering at the marriage gathering. This sterling fellow soon absorbs nearly every chapter until when we get to those days in the Fleet, Mr. Snodgrass, Mr. Winkle, and Mr. Tupman are almost forgotten.

It is easy to point out inconsistencies in Dickens, but one in *Pickwick* I must point out, in order to prove my contention of the essential humanity of Sam Weller.

When Sam first appears, though we know at once that he is an honest, amusing young man, we are given the impression that he has definitely been " rescued" by Mr. Pickwick from an unremunerative and uncongenial job. His forebears, we imagine, did not treat him well and do not deserve good treatment from the author.

There was that shady business over the coach at a former Eatanswill election when Mr. Weller, senior, was bribed to overset some electors. " 'We're all wery fond o' you, Mr. Weller, so in case you *should* have an accident when you're bringing these 'ere woters down, and *should* tip 'em over into the canal vithout 'urtin' of 'em, this for your-self,' says he. 'Gen'lm'n, you're wery kind,' says my father, 'and I'll drink your health in another glass of wine,' says he ; wich he did, and then buttons up the money, and bows himself out." " ' You wouldn't believe, sir,' con-tinued Sam, with a look of inexpressible impudence at his master, ' that on the wery day as he came down with them woters, his coach *was* upset on that 'ere wery spot, and ev'ry man on 'em was turned into the canal.' "

Now I hardly think such behaviour as this is consistent with the dear old male Malaprop to whom we are introduced at various taverns in succeeding pages. It is not at all consistent with that father who brings his money to Mr. Pickwick and says, " 'it ain't o' no use to me. I'm a goin' to vork a coach regular, and han't got noveres to keep it in, unless I vos to pay the guard for takin' care of it, or to put it in vun o' the coach pockets, vich 'ud be a temptation to the insides. If you'll take care of it for me, sir, I shall be wery much obliged to you. P'raps,' said Mr. Weller, walking up to Mr. Pickwick and whispering in his ear, 'p'raps it'll go a little vay towards the expenses of that 'ere conwiction.' "

Yet the words are moving and quite true when we read them, because Mr. Tony Weller has been gradually and skilfully introduced to us. Anything connected with Sam Weller, Dickens took great trouble with, as the character grew on him. Tony Weller is his child's son.

How indifferent Dickens can be to the consistency of his characters is shown in *Pickwick* too. Mr. Perker, like all people connected with the law, seems to be a rather unscrupulous person when he is acting as agent at the Eatanswill election. Later, when he is wanted by Mr. Pickwick in the case of *Bardell* v. *Pickwick*, he is always out. Suddenly when he is wanted by Mr. Dickens to speed up the legal aftermath of the case, he is introduced as an amiable character. But there is none of the subtlety used for the introduction of Mr. Tony Weller. We are merely told that Mr. Perker is an "amiable" or "a good-natured little attorney." Up till now we have come to believe that no Pickwickian attorneys are either amiable or good-natured.

This is fast developing into an undergraduate's Essay on "Dickens, How far was he true to life? Discuss. Write on one side of the paper only." Let us turn back to Sam and get a breath of fresh, gas-lit London fog.

If you walk gently down the declivity from London Bridge station, and turn to your left into a confusion of drays, omnibuses, barrows, and commercial vehicles, you will find yourself (if, indeed, you or I or anyone else can find anyone or anything in that particular Bedlam) in the Borough High Street. Not so far down, before you come to the Marshalsea district where there still seems to hang a foggy gloom from the long demolished debtor's prison, past a few cornchandler's shops and the old-established premises of hop merchants, you will come to a goods yard belonging to the London and North Eastern Railway. And in the goods yard is the George Inn, Southwark, with its galleries and gaslights and boxes of geraniums, its coffee-room with wooden benches. I am sure that this was the Borough Inn to which Jingle flew and where Mr. Pickwick discovered Sam.

It is now the sort of place Americans visit. I suspect that they are the reason of its preservation. But it is a piece of old London that has more merits than mere quaintness, and it is in one of the few parts of London which Sam Weller and Mr. Pickwick would recognise. Possibly if they walked through the city, here and there a church, here and there the name of a tavern would recollect them. But Goswell Street is now the Goswell Road, the little brick houses are mostly demolished, only the squares and crescents of Clerkenwell and Islington survive as Weller knew them.

London may have changed, but London humour is not

dead yet, and Sam Weller and his father may be found any day. Sam takes my fare on the 'bus. When the 'bus is late and the crowd fretful and tired of an evening, Sam's at his most resourceful. Sam, I think it must have been, too, who drove that horse bus in the well-known *Punch* joke made in the days when *Punch* represented English humour. A rich young lady sitting on the front seat on top leant over to the driver as they were going down the Strand, "Do you stop at the Cecil?" she said. "*Do I stop at the Cecil, on twenty-eight bob a week!*" replied Sam Weller.

Mr. Tony Weller is rarer. He is disappearing with the increase of "culture." Long, long ago the pronouncing of "v" as "w" and "w" as "v" died out from Cockneys and now survives only among old-fashioned money-lenders. The misapplication and the mispronunciation of words is dying too. Reasons are obvious, but I am sure that the present "refanement," the aping of what once were considered "genteel" sayings and customs, has nothing to do with the honest reverence of Mr. Tony Weller for what he did not understand.

Tony Wellers are rare. I know one, and am happy to say he is alive still. He was my late father's coachman and my grandfather's before him. I can just remember him driving a brougham pulled by a serviceable grey carriage horse. Motors came in and our Tony Weller was put to driving a motor. Somehow he never cottoned on to it. I used to hear him hissing between his teeth as he cleaned the car; he thought of the car as a horse and would rarely drive it at more than fifteen miles an hour, a good spanking pace, in all conscience.

Once, I remember, he got the car as far as Cornwall.

He had never been to the sea but on a trip to Southend. When he saw a beach surrounded by great cliffs and strewn with rocks, he exclaimed, "Wonderful, sir, ain't it? To think that that was made by 'uman 'ands."

Now he has a job in my father's factory, and still hisses away gently at his work. I think he is one of the best men in the world—better than Tony Weller, but in many ways like him.

The female equivalents of Tony are more common in London. Almost everyone has a few stories showing the humour, unconscious or otherwise, of some inestimable charlady. London clergymen are funds of such stories. A Clerkenwell priest told me the other day of how one of his parishioners was praising a Sister of Mercy in the district, "She's that good she ought to 'ave an inhaler round 'er 'ead."

Education is killing the Tony Wellers of London. But the son is still with us, as the astronomer said when he'd lost the planet he had been looking for. The *Evening News* published a series of Cockney stories last year, among which many Wellerisms may be found. The War brought out the Sam Wellers and Bruce Bairnsfather's "Ole Bill" is typical.

Sam Weller's humour is of a special kind which foreigners do not find funny. It is unsubtle but it is quick. It is generally founded on a true appreciation of other people's character. It exposes humbug, but it is rarely satirical, at the most it is heavily sarcastic:

"Have you been long in Bath, sir?" inquired the powdered-headed footman. "I have not had the pleasure of hearing of you before."

"I haven't created any wery surprisin' sensation here,

as yet," rejoined Sam, "for me and the other fash'nables only come last night."

"Nice place, sir," said the powdered-headed footman.

"Seems so," observed Sam.

"Pleasant society, sir," remarked the powdered-headed footman, "very agreeable servants, sir."

"I should think they wos," replied Sam. "Affable, un-affected, say-nothin'-to-nobody sort o' fellers."

Despite the aloofness of the inhabitants of Bath, Sam's humour managed to get him on. You will remember he was asked to a very exclusive swarry consisting of a select company of the Bath footmen. Sam's Cockney bravado gets him on anywhere. Sam's first meetings with various characters in *Pickwick* are always a treat. There was that delicate mission on which Mr. Pickwick sent him to explore into the Mrs. Bardell situation at Goswell Street. " 'And shut the street door first, please.'

Mr. Weller immediately took the hint; and presenting himself in the parlour, explained his business to Mrs. Bardell thus—

'Wery sorry to 'casion any personal inconwenience, ma'am, as the housebreaker said to the old lady when he put her on the fire; but as me and my governor's only jest come to town, and is jest going away agin, it can't be helped you see.'

'Of course the young man can't help the faults of his master,' said Mrs. Cluppins; much struck by Mr. Weller's appearance and conversation."

By the time the interview was over Sam was having a glass of wine with them all. He said, "that he never could drink before supper, unless a lady drank with him. A great deal of laughing ensued, and Mrs. Sanders volunteered to humour him, so she took a slight sip out of his glass. Then Sam said it must go all round, and they all took a slight sip. Then Mrs. Cluppins proposed a toast, 'Success to Bardell agin Pickwick'; and then the ladies emptied their glasses in honour of the sentiment, and got very talkative directly."

Sam's humorous method of picking up acquaintances everywhere, seems quite spontaneous. It does not smack of the bogus-camaraderie of the modern golf club. There's none of the oily "ole man," "ole top," "what's-yours? Scotch-and-splash- well- ta-ta-'phone- me-some- time-ole-boy"—no, there's none of that, thank heaven. Sam gets on everywhere because he is such a genuine person. Our coachman, whom I was telling you about earlier on, gets on everywhere, too. I remember that when he drove the old car and was left in any country town while we went to lunch at the hotel, there was our coachman, when we came back, in earnest conversation with some new acquaintance. Such a man was Sam.

Sam would not be much of a case for the psychiatrist. He has no complexes. Indeed, an analysis of him boils down instead to an analysis of Dickens's method of presenting humour.

I must say at once that, despite the immortality and all that of *The Pickwick Papers*, Dickens does not make me laugh in the same way as do other humorous writers. The cunning of *The Pickwick Papers* which makes them such grand reading, lies, for me, in their variety—their hundreds of characters, endless situations, some sad, some comical. I use the word comical deliberately. In my own mind, and perhaps in yours, there is subtle difference in the meanings of the words comical and comic. Dickens to me is comical. Dickens is droll. Some other humorists are funny.

78

Primarily I like Dickens for his flow of prose. Not many writers give me more pleasure in literature than Dickens does when he really gets down to a dramatic diatribe, such as that of Fagin's last night alive.

His characters are merely secondary. I am very lucky to have been asked to write about Sam Weller in this book, because Sam is one of the only persons Dickens created as a character who literally becomes as important as the book itself, prose, other characters, situations, and all.

When I look at Sam Weller as drawn by Dickens (not by Phiz) I realise that he appeals to me just as much for his character as for his conversation. This twofold creation is rare in Dickens, whose characters are often either all conversation like Mr. Micawber, or all character like Uriah Heep. That is why it is not unjust to say that Dickens in inventing a great humorous character remains for me more a comical writer than a funny one. I wonder, really, whether it is Sam's humorous activity that makes me delight in him, or whether it is his loyalty and resourcefulness? The incidents connected with Mr. Stiggins have never seemed to me truly comic. They have seemed a little unkind. But that, maybe, is because personally my bias is towards the dimmer offshoots of Calvinism which Mr. Stiggins represents.

The only *incident* in *The Pickwick Papers* which really makes me laugh as an incident is that at the beginning about the stone which is inscribed BILL STUMPS HIS MARK. None of the things Sam Weller does seem to me excruciatingly funny, only the things which he says make me laugh. He acts as a chairman through all the later pages of the book, introducing and filling up the gaps. He is like a chairman at one of the bygone music halls or that gentleman who makes a daily joke at Simpson's (Cheapside) Fish Ordinary.

The Pickwick Papers and Sam Weller are alone in my category of humour. There are three sorts of literary humour which I enjoy; satire, represented by Dryden, Swift, Thackeray, the New Yorker, and some of its imitators, and Evelyn Waugh; parody represented by Horace and James Smith, Hilton, J. W. Stephen, Calverley, and Max Beerbohm; pure humour—Shakespeare, Hood, Edward Lear, Thurber, P. G. Wodehouse. Dickens comes into none of these categories, but he contributes a little to each in *The Pickwick Papers*. Satire he expends on the legal profession. Parody he uses in describing the proceedings of the Pickwick Club at the beginning of the book. Of pure humour Sam Weller is the master. The best example of it is, I think, the story of the crumpets. It is now an hundred years old, but as funny as ever. Told by Dickens it will go on, I hope, for another two hundred years at least.

" 'Wot's the matter?' says the doctor. 'Wery ill,' says the patient. 'Wot have you been a-eatin' on?' says the doctor. 'Roast weal,' says the patient. 'Wot's the last thing you devoured?' says the doctor. 'Crumpets,' says the patient. 'That's it!' says the doctor. 'I'll send you a box of pills directly, and don't you never take no more of 'em,' he says. 'No more o' wot?' says the patient —'pills?' 'No; crumpets,' says the doctor. 'Wy?' says the patient, starting up in bed; 'I've eat four crumpets, ev'ry night for fifteen year, on principle.' 'Well, then, you'd better leave 'em off, on principle,' says the doctor. 'Crumpets is wholesome, sir,' says the patient. 'Crumpets is *not* wholesome, sir,' says the doctor, wery fierce. 'But they're so cheap,' says the patient, comin' down a little, 'and so wery fillin' at the price.' 'They'd be dear to you, at any price; dear if you wos paid to eat 'em,' says the doctor. 'Four crumpets a night,' he says, 'vill do your business in six months!'

The patient looks him full in the face, and turns it over in his mind for a long time, and at last he says, 'Are you sure o' that 'ere, sir?' 'I'll stake my professional reputation on it,' says the doctor. 'How many crumpets, at a sittin,' do you think 'ud kill me off at once?' says the patient. 'I don't know,' says the doctor. 'Do you think half a crown's wurth 'ud do it?' says the patient. 'I think it might,' says the doctor. 'Three shillin's' wurth 'ud be sure to do it, I s'pose?' says the patient. 'Certainly,' says the doctor. 'Wery good,' says the patient; 'good-night.' Next mornin' he gets up, has a fire lit, orders in three shillin's' wurth o' crumpets, toasts 'em all, eats 'em all, and blows his brains out."

Let me advise those who have not taken the walk before, to walk through the leisurely extravagant pages of *Pickwick*. Let those who have taken the walk already take it again, they will find every variety of humour, every generous emotion of which the soul is capable on the way, but they will find in Sam Weller an epitome of the whole book.

TONY WELLER

By Bransby Williams

VI

URING my many journeys across the world in ships I have made friends with several great captains and learned from them that they believed their good ships had souls—that to them they were living things who knew what was expected of them and answered to their captain's call.

A hundred years ago a youth just twenty-four years of age created a ship called *The Pickwick Papers* whose many passengers carried much happiness to the ports of mankind all over the world. Little did that young man dream that he would captain so many other famous ships and have such wonderful passenger lists, totalling at his death nearly two thousand. But he believed in himself, his ships and his passengers, the latter because he had met them in life and subconsciously had taken mental snapshots on his highly sensitised brain.

And here we are to-day celebrating the hundredth anniversary of the launching of that wonderful ship *Pickwick*. The beginning of that voyage was not propitious. It was not at first realised what a grand ship she was, and, moreover, before she could reach the open waters she lost her chief officer—Robert Seymour. But presently Sam Weller joined the crew, and thenceforth the ship had a good "sale-ing" wind.

But we will drop the metaphor. The romantic story of the birth of this masterpiece is well known. At first the sales were disappointing; the death of the artist Seymour was a grave set-back; the non-success of R. W. Buss, who

The Valentine.

was chosen to succeed him, was another factor which threatened failure. And then came Sam Weller, and with him came "Phiz." Thenceforth all was well, and *Pickwick* became the most triumphant success in the history of English literature.

There are far abler pens than mine writing of, and to, their old friends, conjuring up for others their thoughts and memories of their first meetings and lasting friendship. I am allotted the pleasant task of penning my poor words to old Tony Weller—would that I could borrow the magic pen of his creator, Charles Dickens, to do justice to this old giant—for assuredly he *was* a giant among stage coachmen.

"How are you? Wery glad to see you, and hope our acquaintance 'll be a long 'un, as the gen'l'man said to the fi'pun note." Was it you who said that, or was it that son of yours, Samivel? (spell it with a "wee" to please you!) Tony, my old friend, our acquaintance has been a long one now. May it continue till my dying day—and then shall we meet again on Olympus? For you are immortal, are you not?

I call you Tony, you see. Your son was not always so respectful, was he? Did he not call you at various times "My ancient," "The old 'un," "Nobs," "Fireworks," "Prooshian Blue," and "My Father!"

Well, dear old friend, here I am, an actor who has dared many times to attempt to impersonate you. You caused me many hours of thought and anxiety—how to get your voice, your face, your figure, and how to clothe that figure correctly. In the matter of clothing though, I was fortunate enough to find during my wanderings a real old coachman's coat, complete with its many capes. What a weight to carry! You with your avoirdupois and the great coat and shawls added would certainly break down some of our modern weighing machines!

I am pleased to say, Tony, that the public certainly received my impersonation with great joy all over the world—in America, Africa, Australia, New Zealand, Canada, and all over Great Britain.

During the Great War I was false to you, and impersonated your son Samivel's guv'nor, Mr. Pickwick. I got together replicas of the Club and we drove on a coach through London. You were there, but your impersonator on that occasion did not need any padding such as I had to use. He was, and is, a fine, unctuous Shakespearian actor named Roy Byford, who has since been successful as Shakespeare's Fat Man, viz. Falstaff.

How the public welcomed that sight in the streets during that painful and anxious time! On another occasion I sat on the Empire Stage as Pickwick surrounded by the members of the Club, and the "Samivel" on that occasion was John Le Hay. But the great occasion was when I presented a Dickens's Fair in the Botanical Gardens and there had a large tent for the Pickwickians, and again John Le Hay was the Sam Weller who sang all day long. I did all these things to raise funds for the wounded and to found a home in your creator's name at St. Leonards for the blinded soldiers and sailors, and my efforts were blessed by our Compassionate Saviour.

Here I am, Tony, alone at night after I have left the "garish footlights," those lights that your creator mentioned at the close of his last public reading.

I am alone with my thoughts and memories. Your clothes are hanging in the Theatre Dressing Room, but your spirit is here with me. All are sleeping, only the tick of the clock (not Master Humphreys) accompanies the scratch of my pen.

Dear old Tony, you were a rough diamond, yet I think a fine old English gentleman in nature at any rate, and that is what really matters. It has been said that your prototype was an old chap called "Old Chumley," but Charles Dickens during his many journeys as a Reporter must have seen you often and put you "on his list." We are grateful to him for making you known to us. It is said that "all great things are simple." If that is so you are a great soul in your honesty and simplicity. That you were a good old coachman and understood your horses we know. Indeed you held that a knowledge of horses was the be-all and end-all. Did you not once say: "The man as can form a ackerate judgment of a animal can form a ackerate judgment of anythin' "? You were elemental in your outlook, but the elements are first things, are they not? You believed in a simple bringing up of your son Samivel, for instance, you let him run the streets, believing it was "the only way to make a boy sharp." Such methods would not meet with the approval of our present day educationists, but they succeeded in your case, for Sam was sharp on the uptake of almost anything and always had a ready and witty answer, while he had your own qualities of integrity and loyalty. You were a philosopher, too. I remember that Sam told Mr. Pickwick—"Philosophy is very much in my father's line. If my mother-in-law blows him up, he whistles—she flies in a passion and breaks his pipe; he steps out, and gets another. Then she screams wery loud and falls into 'sterics'; he smokes wery comfort-ably till she comes to agin. That's philosophy, Sir, ain't it?"

Do you remember giving Mr. Pickwick your wonderful cure for the gout? "I've found a sov'rin cure for the gout. The gout is a complaint as arises from too much ease and comfort. If ever you're attacked with the gout, Sir, jest you marry a widder as has got a good loud woice, with a decent notion of usin' it, and you'll never have the gout agin. It's a capital prescription, sir. I takes it reg'lar, and I can warrant it drive away any illness as is caused by too much jollity."

You certainly were not as sharp as your son in worldly matters or you would never have married that aforesaid "widder." But your very simplicity betrayed you then! As you have told us, "there never was a nicer woman as a widder than that second wentur o' mine, a sweet creetur she was, and it's a great pity she ever changed her condition——" But you learned your lesson! From that time on you warned all and sundry "Beware o' Widders." Even after her death you were afraid to be left alone with any woman, in case she was a widder, and would be a "marryin' of you." But, dear old Tony, you were true to your widder and very patient as we know so well. How you detested that borrowing, drinking, hypocritical Stiggins, tho' you certainly did admire his power of suction.

You had a contempt for the tea meetings and tea drinkings at the Brick Lane Mission, and simple as you were, you held decided views on foreign missions. You did not believe in "Flannel Veskits" for young niggers, or the women wasting time making clothes for "copper-coloured niggers as don't want 'em and taking no notice of flesh-coloured Christians as do." There are many to-day, one hundred years after your famous utterance, who agree with you. Negroes in their own hot countries do not need "Veskits," while many thousands of poorly clad and hungry British men, women, and children do need them. How much better it would be if charity commenced at home, and missionaries remained there and worked there!

Your wife, poor soul, admitted on her death-bed that she had made a mistake—not in marrying you, but in her conduct as your wife. Too late, she admitted that you were a kind-hearted man and that she might have made you more "comfortabler." You, kind soul that you were, did not taunt her with her failures, but comforted her and told her she had been a "werry good wife." Thousands all over the world think of you only as a great fat old humorist— a rough, unlettered, comic old coachman—but they don't know you as they should. You were a philosopher and you were more than that. You were a *gentleman*, Tony. Your chivalry to your dying wife, your genuine sorrow at her death—"But she died after all"—show that. Unlettered? Yes, yes, but what man of culture ever achieved anything greater than your letter to Sam after your wife's death?

"She was turnin' the corner—she took the wrong road and vent downhill with a welocity you never see. . . . She paid the last pike at twenty minutes afore six o'clock yesterday evening—having done the journey werry much under the reg'lar time vich praps was partly owen to her haven taken in werry little luggage. . . . Come and see me, Sammy . . . for I'm werry lonely, infernally yours, Tony Veller."

Your wife bequeathed you eleven hundred and eighty pounds. Did you spend it on yourself? No, dear old Tony. You decided to put it "someveres safe." You told Mr. Pickwick "I'm goin' to vork a coach reg'lar. . . . If you'll take care on it for me, sir, I shall be wery much obliged." Then you showed not only your kindness of heart and great simplicity, but the true fineness of your make-up, for you believed Mr. Pickwick to be needing money to pay his damages in the recent breach of promise proceedings. "Pr'aps it'll go a little vay towards the expenses of that 'ere conwiction," you whispered. "All I can say is just keep it till I ask you for it again." And not waiting for thanks you ran out of the room "with a celerity scarcely to be expected from so corpulent a subject." Nothing comic about that, Tony. Just sweet humanity—and the world loved and still loves you for it.

How surprised you were when you discovered Samivel writing a love letter and sending a "Walentine"—"I didn't think you'd a done it, I didn't think you'd a done it, Sammy. . . . It's a dreadful trial to a father's feelin's, Sammy." But after lighting your pipe and a double glass of the "inwariable" you settled comfortably down ready to offer your advice—"Fire away." The moment Sam began with "lovely creetur" you were alarmed that it might be poetry. "Poetry's unnat'ral; no man ever talked poetry. . . . I never know'd a respectable coachman as wrote poetry, 'cept one, and he was hung for highway robbery; and *he* was only a Camberwell man, so even that's no rule."

When the letter was disposed of you next gave Sam your legal opinion that nothing could save his guvnor but a "alleybi," and you stuck to your opinion. At the end of the trial, when Mr. Pickwick had lost his case and was mulcted in heavy damages, you wore a mournful expression and said, "I know'd what 'ud come o' this here mode o' doing bisness. Oh, Sammy, Sammy, vy worn't there a alleybi?"

I remember many years ago, at a meeting at the Mansion House in London, standing with the late Lord Rosebery and Bishop Welldon. The Bishop said—"I place the *Tale of Two Cities* next my Bible." Lord Rosebery said—"Yes, Dickens taught us great sympathy, but how he did teach us to laugh."

Tony, we've laughed at you and with you—more often *with* you, for you were indeed a great "laugher" yourself.

It has been said that Charles Dickens was a greater character creator than novelist, and that his books were one long procession of characters. I am not certain as to the date, but there was once a Dickens production in Paris—a sort of version of "Oliver Twist"—the author got somewhat mixed, for Mr. Micawber visited Fagin's den in order to rescue young Oliver. This causes me to think. Suppose you, old Tony, had been introduced into other books in the same way that Jeffrey Farnol reintroduces characters such as "Jasper Shrig'" into several stories, you might have driven other coaches. I wonder what you would have said and done to Mr. Wackford Squeers when he took his poor half-starved victims on the coach to Dothe Boys Hall? I think your great, big sympathetic heart would have made you repeat your treatment of Stiggins and give him "one for his nob" and put his head in the first horse trough you approached. What conversations we might have heard if you had driven Mr. and Mrs. Micawber and the twins to Canterbury! How your heart would have been touched had you been driving along the Dover Road, and had seen poor little David trudging his weary way, after selling his coat and waistcoat.

Had you been driving back to London on the Great North Road or from St. Albans you might have seen that pathetic sickly waif, "Poor Jo," dragging his feeble body to London to die near the only man who "was wery good to me he was." I can almost see you, Tony, standing bare-headed as dear Old Snagsby repeated the Lord's Prayer for Jo, and hear you in your own uneducated way saying those words:

"Dead, your Majesty, Dead, my Lords and gentlemen, Dead, Right Reverends and Wrong Reverends of every order. Dead, men and women, born with Heavenly compassion in your hearts. And dying thus around us every day."

Here indeed was one of your poor flesh-coloured Christians—dying neglected at home.

It would have been interesting and "jolly" to have heard you and Mark Tapley and Martin Chuzzlewit had you driven them from Salisbury to London, when they were going to emigrate to America. Certainly, both you and Mark would have "come out strong."

Talking of Salisbury reminds one of Mr. Pecksniff. I can see the expression on your face, had you been near by when he declared—"What are we but coaches? Some of us are slow coaches; some of us are fast coaches. Our passions are the horses; and rampant animals too! We start from the 'Mother's Arms' and we run to the 'Dust Shovel'."

It would have been interesting to have heard you talking with dear old Captain Cuttle. You would have compared your "widder" with his landlady, Mrs. Macstinger.

How you would have chuckled had you been driving the little runaways, Master Harry Walmers and his sweetheart, little Miss Norah—I daresay you would have found some good "advice" for them.

But you had been introduced to us before any of these characters had been born—you were just driving on ahead of this glorious pageant.

Were you able to visit us to-day you would see some wonderful improvements in the great highways, but I'm afraid you would snort at the great rush of cars and have something trenchant to say about some of the thoughtless drivers, for we know your opinion of the coming of the railway train: you said it "was unconstitootional and an inwaser o' privileges." How your old spirit must haunt the occasional coach when driven down to Brighton or Richmond!

The time came when you had to retire, and unfortunately you got the gout and were not able to put into practice your "sov'rin cure" for the widder with the loud "woice" was silent and had gone aloft.

When Mr. Pickwick inquired about your health you told him "The axle ain't broke yet. We keeps up a steady pace, not too sewere, but with a moderate degree o' friction, and the consekens is that ve're still running and comes to time reglar." For all the gout, how proud you were when you were able to announce: "Sam conferred on me the ancient title of grandfather, vich has long laid dormouse and supposed to be hextinct in our family." How proud you were of little Tony! When at the age of four and a half you wanted to dispose of his "petticuts" and dress him as you thought he should be dressed in "a little white hat and a little sprig Weskit, and little knee cords and little top boots, and a little green coat with little bright buttons, and a little welwet collar— That's the costoom and once make sich a model on him as that, and you'd say he was a angel." It was a good thing for you, Tony, that Mr. Pickwick had so well invested the contents of your pocket-book that you had a handsome independence to retire on. Thus you were a happy old gentleman, full of pride in your son and your grandson, though troubled with the gout, and though the dread of widders never left you. The London that you and Sam and Mr. Pickwick knew has almost disappeared, not only the buildings, but the spirit of those days. Now all is rush and hustle, but we love to remember those days, and when we have shuffled off "this mortal coil" our children and their children will read the *Pickwick Papers*, and in their fancy you will still be the same honest, cheery, loving old soul to them that you have been to us and our fathers. In their fancy they will see you mount your box and hear the horses rattle their harness—"Now, Villam, run 'em out." Away you will go on your coach rattling over the cobble-stones "to admiration of the whole population." So, dear old Tony, I must leave you; the old clock is ticking away.

In this review of your life and character I am more drawn to you than ever. The world loved you when you first appeared—you endeared yourself to us, full of humour and loving kindness. We love you and your companions to-day—a hundred years young—Good-bye, or, as you would say, "Adoo"—your shadow fades before me, but your memory will outlive and outlast us, for, as Mr. Chesterton has said, you are of the stuff that fairies are made of.

JINGLE
By Alec Waugh

VII

MAX BEERBOHM is invariably in his happiest vein when he is caricaturing George Moore, whether with pen or pencil. The "Dickens" chapter in *A Christmas Garland* is one of his most quoted essays. George Moore's imaginary conversion is very typical of the man whose abrupt changes of allegiance made life an adventure for him long after his seventieth year was passed: the man who boasted of the little rather than the amount that he had read, who maintained that "to appreciate a few things fully, you must let many dishes pass," could scarcely have been parodied more aptly and more affectionately.

"There never was a writer except Dickens. Perhaps you have never heard say of him? No matter, till a few days past he was only a name to me. I remember that when I was a young man in Paris, I read a praise of him in some journal; but in those days I was kneeling at other altars, I was scrubbing other doorsteps. . . . There is but one doorstep worth scrubbing. The doorstep of Charles Dickens. . . .

"Did he write many books? I know not, it does not greatly matter, he wrote *The Pickwick Papers*; that suffices. I have read as yet but one chapter, describing a Christmas party in a country house. Strange that anyone should have essayed to write about anything but that! Christmas—I see it now—is the only moment in which men and women are really alive, are really worth writing about. . . ."

Discovery of Jingle in the Fleet.

It is parody at its best, and how typical of Moore is the passage that almost immediately follows.

"To have described divinely a Christmas party is something, but it is not everything. The disengaging of the erotic motive is everything, is the only touchstone. . . . Dickens disengages the erotic motive through two figures, Mr. Winkle, a sportsman, and Miss Arabella, 'a young lady with fur-topped boots'. . . ."

A Christmas Garland was published, it must be remembered, in 1910, at a time when the circulating libraries were busy over the banning of novels that seem singularly blameless now. The war for freedom of expression was being waged with Abyssinian savagery. Quarter was neither given nor expected. Speech after speech, article after article protested against the handicap under which the English novelist was forced to struggle. "What a novelist, for example, might not Dickens have been," they argued, "had he been allowed the same freedom that Balzac enjoyed in France." Such arguments were natural and effective weapons, when the stress of battle was at its height, when the issue was uncertain. At such a time the idea of George Moore disentangling the erotic motive in *The Pickwick Papers* was irresistibly amusing.

But the best jokes, even as the best wines, to accept Moore's own simile, acquire and lose merit, and the jest at the expense of Winkle, or rather at the expense of Dickens's extreme propriety has lost something of its topicality. For the fight for freedom of expression has been, if not actually won, at least fought to a point where all save the most Chauvinist diehard is ready to declare an armistice. *Lady Chatterley's Lover* may have been driven to subterranean circulation, but it is on the shelves of anyone who wants to read it. And no one in 1915, when *The Rainbow* was being burnt, could have believed that within twenty years *Appointment in Samara* would be in library circulation. Before the War, a relationship was considered to be platonic unless the writer specifically stated that it was not: to-day a relationship is held to be unplatonic, unless the heroine's powers of resistance are not only stated but explained. The novelist of to-day enjoys within reasonable limits complete freedom of expression. The fight is as good as won. And the novelist is asking, as the victor always tends to do, when the first flush of "after-battle wine" has lost its potency, how much actually has been gained. How much better off is he than his Victorian predecessors? Because he can use certain words, describe in detail certain actions, is it really any easier for him to present his characters four square? Was Thackeray right when he maintained that since Fielding it had not been possible to draw an honest picture of a man? May he not have placed too high a value on the freedom he was denied? The modern novelist re-reads novels that were written under conditions of close censorship. Has the power of the siren anywhere been drawn more wooingly than in *Spring Floods?* Has a marriage based solely upon physical attraction been ever more unmistakably diagnosed than it was by Tolstoi in the first section of *War and Peace?* The modern novelist is forced to wonder whether it was so much the limitations of their own age as of their own natures that made so many of the major Victorian novelists shirk even oblique references to a tabooed subject. The Russians managed well enough. So for that matter did the Victorian poets. Browning said what he had to say, and said it clearly. Dickens could have, if he had really wanted.

These thoughts occurred to me, as for the purposes of my contribution to this symposium I was re-reading the "Jingle" passages in *The Pickwick Papers*.

In the *Dickens Dictionary* Jingle is labelled as "an impudent, strolling actor, who palms himself off as a gentleman of consequence, sponges good dinners and borrows money, and finally gets into the Fleet prison, where Mr. Pickwick finds him in great destitution and distress, and benevolently pays his debts and releases him on satisfactory evidence of penitence, and on promise of reformation which is faithfully carried out. Mr. Jingle is a very loquacious person, rarely speaking a connected sentence, but stringing together mere disjointed phrases, generally without verbs."

He is that of course; but he is far more than that. His creator wrote of him to Catherine Hogarth: "I have at this moment got Pickwick and his friends on the Rochester coach, and they are going on swimmingly in company with a very different character from any I have yet described, who I flatter myself will make a decided hit."

It was a prophecy amply to be fulfilled. Jingle is one of the great comic characters in literature. He is moreover not only one of those characters who are alive from their first entrance, but who become more alive with each fresh appearance. He bustles on to the stage at a moment of drama, to rescue Mr. Pickwick from embarrassment. He is wearing clothes that are described in extensive detail, clothes of a kind on which the eye of no mortal now alive has rested: that does not matter. He is clear, unmistakable to the mind's eye, "thin and haggard, with his incredible air of jaunty impudence and perfect self-possession." He begins to talk with his "gift o' the gab wery gallopin'."

A great many writers have made their characters talk in sharp, jerky, verbless sentences. But no one has employed that particular device with such effect. "Eye damaged, sir? Waiter! Raw beef-steak for the gentleman's eye—nothing like raw beef-steak for a bruise, sir. Cold lamp-post very good, but lamp-post inconvenient—damned odd standing in the open street half an hour, with your eye against a lamp-post—eh—very good—ha! ha!" Within a page and a half the reader has begun to laugh with him, and to like him; to recognise him as a friend.

That feeling of friendship never slackens. Within a page Jingle has jumped on to the coach, leaving the settling of the bill to another's charge. The reader suspects he is a rogue. But his affection grows. Another minute and Jingle is relating an absurd anecdote about a dog: so he is a liar too. The page is turned and he has revealed himself as an unabashed sensualist. "English girls not so fine as Spanish—noble creatures—jet hair—black eyes—lovely forms—sweet creatures—beautiful." The coach rattles up to the Bull Inn, and with calm effrontery he does the one thing that every one of us has at some moment longed to do and dared not: ordered his own dinner of his host. "Great pleasure—not presume to dictate but broiled fowl and mushrooms—capital thing! What time?" Before Jingle has sat down to that broiled fowl, the reader is ready to travel in his company through the nine hundred pages of the Pickwick Chronicle.

The reader is happy in his company. Jingle is a rogue. The wrath of the Wellers, the Wardles, and Mr. Pickwick is amply earned. But the reader is always on his side. The reader wants him to come off best. Just as the reader chuckles over the absurd account of the cricket match against Colonel Blazo, so does he chuckle over Mr. Pickwick's discomfiture at the hands of the young ladies' seminary, so does he chuckle over the effrontery with which Jingle relieves Mr. Wardle of a hundred and twenty pounds: and at the insolence of that final gesture when he tosses the licence at Mr. Pickwick's feet. "Here, get the name altered—take home the lady—do for Tuppy." Whenever Jingle appears upon the scene, the reader prepares to enjoy himself. Jingle is always in character. Yet each time he manages to go one better. Admirable as is his duel with Mr. Wardle's attorney, he is still better when faced in Mr. Nupkins with a more redoubtable opponent.

"What prevents me," said Mr. Nupkins, "from detaining these men as rogues and impostors? It is foolish mercy. What prevents me?"

"Pride, old fellow, pride," replied Jingle quite at his ease. "Wouldn't do—no go—caught a captain, eh?—ha! ha! very good—husband for daughter—biter bit—make it public—not for worlds—look stupid—very!"

Jingle knows his world so well: he plays upon its vanity, its baseness, its snobbery, its avarice. It is only because human beings are vain and petty that he can live so successfully upon his wits. That in part is why we love him: in the main we love him because he makes us laugh, but in part because he exploits what is despicable in human nature: because he humbles pomposity and pretence.

In part, too, we love him because he never snivels. Even in the Fleet prison his head is high. "No danger of overwalking yourself here—spike park—grounds pretty—romantic but not extensive—open for public inspection—family always in town—housekeeper desperately careful—very." He is in desperate straits. But one knows that he will come out safe. One suspects that his old enemy will prove his rescuer. He receives the news of his release as one would expect. Of course he will justify his benefactor's faith. "Not lost—pay it all—stick to business—cash up—every farthing. Yellow fever perhaps—can't help that—if not——" We know him so well that we know exactly what happened to him in the land of opportunity. Settle down to work? build up a fortune? But of course not. He would live by his wits still: marry an American: an heiress: a young one of great beauty, and, what is more, make her extremely happy, without ever letting her suspect that he was exceedingly unfaithful to her, after the manner of Casanovas.

For that is the point about Jingle. Though he is watered down for Victorian consumption, he is the adventurer who makes his living out of women. And that is a type that is definitely not platonic. Though this fact is never stated, it is as clear to the reader as if the long score of his conquests had been recited. There is all the difference in the world between that two line speech about Spanish women and Tupman's allegiance to "the fair sex." You can picture Tuppy in some tap-room toasting "to our wives and sweethearts; may they never meet." Dickens knew well enough the type that he was drawing. In Jingle more than in any character in Dickens's novels there is the proof that had he wanted, Dickens could in spite of the reticence of his age, have written truthfully of love. But in Jingle there is also the proof that it was not that reticence, but the limitations of his own temperament that prevented him. In Jingle more than anywhere else is his dislike of women, in particular his cruelty to old women, definitely underlined.

Arnold Bennett has described how the idea of *The Old Wives' Tale* came to him from the glimpse across a restaurant of an old humpy woman, and the recognition that she had been once young with a heart opened to affection. That is a sensation of which Dickens would have been incapable. An old woman was always ridiculous. He could never have written of Miss Harriet, as Maupassant did, with tenderness. There is no suspicion of pity for Jingle's victims: no recognition of the fact that while the discomfiture of Mr. Nupkins is intrinsically funny, the exploitation of Miss Wardle's faded feelings is definitely not. Dickens could not have written well of love, because he was not at heart a lover, in the sense, for example, that Browning was. He could write of young love in *David Copperfield*, and in *Our Mutual Friend* of dour and sulky passion. But his cruelty to women is of the kind that is impossible to the man who has been happy by them. I should doubt if Dickens ever was. I should doubt if he ever really relaxed to love, if he could have understood Macheath's song "When the mind of a man . . .": if the phrase "there's nothing unbends the mind like them" meant more than the bare words. In Dickens's love letters, published a few months ago, there is no real sense of intimacy.

It has been said that Dickens described only the surface of life. That is not true, I think. He described the brave pageant of life: its noise, its bustle, its colour, its changing scenes. He loved it, and he saw to the heart of it. He always saw to the heart of what he loved. But love, yes, that I think he did describe from the outside, and in an almost hostile spirit. Some men find in love escape from the business and strain of living: some few find a harmony between the two. Others find escape from an ill-adjusted personal life in the sounding and wide arena. Dickens was one of them. I do not think that, with his temperament, he would have written so very differently had he been in our uncensoring age.

MR WARDLE

By Walter Dexter

VIII

STRAWS, so the weather-worn proverb remarks, show how the wind blows; and it is a fine gentle wind, hardly more than a puff, which, quite early in the adventures of the Pickwickians, wafts us in the direction of what is probably the truest drawn, and certainly the most lovable, character in the book, the jovial, hale and hearty Mr. Wardle.

It happened this way. Mr. Pickwick, jostled by the military at the review on Chatham lines, lost his hat. It "rolled sportively" before a gentle wind. "The wind puffed, and Mr. Pickwick puffed, and the hat rolled over and over as merrily as a lively porpoise in a strong tide; and on it might have rolled, far beyond Mr. Pickwick's reach, had not its course been providentially stopped." And so, just as fortunately, we are brought into the presence of "a stout old gentleman" with a jolly red face shining with smiles and health. He was standing "in an open barouche, with a hamper of spacious dimensions fastened up behind"; and just in case this is not a sufficiently good introduction to the hospitable old fellow, we are told that the hamper was of the kind "which always awakens in a contemplative mind, associations connected with cold fowls, tongues, and bottles of wine." Against the wheels of this carriage Mr. Pickwick's hat came to rest just as he was on the point of giving up the chase. He had only just planted the recovered property on his head once again when he and his friends who had by this time joined him were greeted with a hearty welcome from the self-same

Mr. Wardle & his friends under the influence of the Salmon.

old gentleman: "Come along, sir, pray come up. . . . Very glad to see you; know you very well, gentlemen, though you mayn't remember me."

It strikes me forcibly there are many people who "mayn't remember" him, so overshadowed has Mr. Wardle become by his own immortal Fat Boy, to say nothing of Mr. Pickwick, the two Wellers and Serjeant Buzfuz, and a host of others. For Mr. Wardle is a "straight" part, and Dickens is best remembered by his "characters." And so in this great galaxy of *The Pickwick Papers* we are apt to overlook this true portrait of a fine old English gentleman; yet he would make a notable centre figure in a book less generously loaded with great and lasting characters.

The simple, downright words of his greeting are indicative of Mr. Wardle. With such skill is the character drawn with very few words, that here he is before our eyes, introducing us to his maiden sister and his two charming daughters, "a stout old gentleman in blue coat with bright buttons, breeches, and top-boots" with a beaming smile and hearty laugh. His recognition is so sincere that he soon becomes "out of breath with his own anticipation of pleasure." As typical a John Bull as ever a novelist created.

It is not very long before he invites his newly made friends to visit him at his country house, and as this type of country gentleman is never seen to better advantage than in his own country seat, we follow him; recalling his parting words:

"I don't let you off, mind, under a week; and undertake that you shall see everything that is worth seeing. If you've come down for a country life, come to me, and I'll give you plenty of it."

Such was Mr. Wardle's welcome to Manor Farm, Dingley Dell.

2

Where is this Dingley Dell in which Mr. Wardle's ancestral home was situated? A natural question, surely, after we have read the charming description of it, and the delightful happenings connected with it.

"There ain't a better spot o' ground in all Kent, sir," was the assertion, twice repeated, of the "hard headed man with the pippin face"; and who would be prepared to contradict him? Yet where is this truly delightful and most hospitable domain to be found?

Its very name is captivating—Dingley Dell. *The Pickwick Papers* is essentially a novel of travel. We started from Goswell Street, passed St. Martin's-le-Grand, and first of all arrived at the Golden Cross at Charing Cross. Then in company with Mr. Pickwick and his three friends we took coach for Rochester; with them we admired the view as we crossed the bridge, and stopped at the Bull Inn in the High Street to recall the adventures in the ball-room, and the bedrooms occupied by the party, including the identical communicating rooms incidental to the scene on the staircase where Dr. Slammer challenged Mr. Jingle to a duel. We have been out on Chatham Lines, where Mr. Wardle made his first appearance, and seen Fort Pitt, where the duel would have been fought had not Dr. Slammer discovered at the last moment that Mr. Winkle was not the man who had insulted him. Then we have come with the Pickwickians in that "curious little green box on four wheels with a low place like a wine bin for two behind and an elevated perch for one in front, drawn by an immense brown horse displaying great symmetry of bone"; and have laughed at Mr. Winkle's misadventures with the horse that would persist in going sideways, and sympathised with the party on their enforced walk to Manor Farm: and now we are at an entire loss to say where Dingley Dell really is.

It is all very exasperating. The neighbouring town of Muggleton is also "wropt in mystery," and we realise it is a curious fact that although Dickens describes by name a dozen or more actual places in London, and is quite precise about Rochester, Cobham, Ipswich, Bury St. Edmunds, Bath, Bristol, Birmingham, and Towcester, only three places, Dingley Dell, Muggleton, and Eatanswill, are completely disguised; and two of them are in Kent, the county he knew best of all.

We can therefore rightly surmise that, as Robert Langton pointed out in 1883 in *The Childhood and Youth of Dickens*, Manor Farm, Dingley Dell, was entirely a creation of his fancy, and discard the later assertion of Percy Fitzgerald in his *Life of Dickens* (1905) that it was "a positive certainty" that Dickens in his youth had visited "Manor Farm, near Maidstone," one Christmas time, and reproduced some twenty years later, in chapter twenty-eight of the novel, his recollection of the joyous time he had there. Certainly that chapter is arrested for a moment for the following charming retrospect, but that does not necessarily mean that Dickens was drawing on any one particular recollection, as Fitzgerald would have us believe.

How many old recollections, and how many dormant sympathies, does Christmas awaken!

We write these words now, many miles distant from the spot at which, year after year, we met on that day, a merry and joyous circle. Many of the hearts that throbbed so gaily then, have ceased to beat; many of the looks that shone so brightly then, have

ceased to glow; the hands we grasped, have grown cold; the eyes
we sought, have hid their lustre in the grave; and yet the old
house, the room, the merry voices and smiling faces, the jest, the
laugh, the most minute and trivial circumstance connected with
those happy meetings, crowd upon our mind at each recurrence
of the season, as if the last assemblage had been but yesterday.
Happy, happy Christmas, that can win us back to the delusions of
our childish days, that can recall to the old man the pleasures of
his youth, and transport the sailor and the traveller, thousands of
miles away, back to his own fire-side and his quiet home!

However, the identification of Dickens' landmarks is a
very fascinating pursuit, and after carefully analysing every
word of description, and measuring certain roads and by-
paths, old and experienced topographers like William R.
Hughes the Birmingham Librarian, during "A Week's
Tramp in Dickensland," in 1891, and Fred G. Kitton, who
accompanied him, stated that Cob Tree at Sandling "may
justly be considered as the prototype of Manor Farm."
But against that we have to place the later researches of
Mr. S. J. Rust, a native of the district, who in *The Dickensian* for 1926 (p. 225) proved with conviction that
Birling Place fitted the story much better than Cob Tree.
Either this is a coincidence or a proof that Dickens had no
particular place in mind when introducing Manor Farm
into his story, otherwise there would have been no object
in being so indefinite in his locality.

We must therefore put aside the possibility that the
owner of Cob Tree in 1836, a certain William Spong, at
that time forty-seven years of age, was the original of Mr.
Wardle, although his age, and undoubted good hearted-
ness, might have fitted him for the part. Dickens, of course,
drew from life, but to seek to prove that he had a living
model for each one of his characters, is to relegate him to

the place assigned to him by one of his critics, that of a "glorified reporter" instead of asserting his position as a great creator of characters.

3

Mr. Wardle is almost always referred to by that simple designation. The "Mr." befits his character. In such dignified way he was always addressed by his tenants. We are never informed if he possessed any other name, but the registers of the old Church nearby would surely tell us if we made a search. The only other appellations he receives are "hearty" and "old," the latter never used in a derogatory sense, but always with affection. Mr. Wardle was by no means old in years, although to his young creator, only just passed his twenty-fourth birthday, he may have appeared so. His mother, "a very old lady," so described, was on the authority of her lawyer, less than seventy-three years of age. Her daughter was "fifty, if you're an hour," according to Mr. Wardle himself; he would most probably know, as she was older than he; hence it is quite likely he was well under fifty.

"Hearty" by all means, but certainly not "old." Just remember how he disported himself on the ice at Christmas time, when "with the impetuosity which characterised all his proceedings," he dragged off his skates and "went down the slide with a rapidity which came very close upon Mr. Weller and beat the Fat Boy all to nothing!"

And this, remember, after he had been reported as out of breath "by reason of the indefatigable manner in which he had converted his legs into a pair of compasses and drawn complicated problems on the ice."

Then, too, we must not forget the famous walk of five-and-twenty miles undertaken by the men at his own instigation, between the wedding breakfast and the dinner in order "to get rid of the effects of the wine" at that ceremonial feast; and of the times he is described as "running upstairs" at Osborne's Hotel in the Adelphi. Most decidedly not old in the usual acceptance of that word as applied to age.

He was a widower—of how long standing we do not know—and he appears to have been quite content to remain so, although he seems to have had an eye on the "black-eyed little flirt" Arabella Allen, if we are to believe him when he told Mr. Pickwick he'd "a great idea of marrying her himself one of these days"; but as that was after Mr. Winkle's successful capture of her, we may take this as a joking remark on the old fellow's part.

He was deeply attached to his two girls, Bella and Emily. The former married the nondescript Mr. Trundle, the man of one single speech; and against the father's will too; but he was too good-natured to stand in the way of his daughter's happiness. "I would never force a young girl's inclinations," he said. It was the same when he heard of his second daughter's attachment for Snodgrass; he dismissed the plans he had formed for a rich young suitor, and with the proverbial "God bless you, my children," bestowed a handsome portion on her.

But he was, for the once, "testy" when he heard of it first of all, and then "inflammable." He "went off into a passion" and "frightened his mother into a fit," and fretted and fumed and made a great disturbance, and it took all the wiles of Mrs. Winkle, née Arabella Allen, to bring him to the point when he was once more "overflowing with hilarity and kindness."

His mother and sister completed the household. We are introduced to the former wearing "a lofty cap and faded silk gown" sitting in

the post of honour on the right-hand corner of the chimney piece; and various certificates of her having been brought up in the way she should go when young, and of her not having departed from it when old, ornamented the walls, in the form of samplers of ancient date, worsted landscapes of equal antiquity, and crimson silk tea-kettle holders of a more modern period. The aunt, the two young ladies, and Mr. Wardle, each vying with the other in paying zealous and unremitting attentions to the old lady, crowded round her easy chair, one holding her ear-trumpet, another an orange, and a third a smelling-bottle, while a fourth was busily engaged in patting and punching the pillows which were arranged for her support.

As we see, Mr. Wardle's attention to his mother was most dutiful; "unremitting," says Dickens, and so it was. Towards his sister Rachel, otherwise referred to as "the spinster aunt," Mr. Wardle was always tolerant. "She's a Miss, she is; and yet she ain't a Miss" was his introduction of her to Mr. Pickwick. She might certainly have "paired off" with that gentleman, but evidently Dickens was reserving both for less conventional destinies.

4

"Welcome to Manor Farm," was Mr. Wardle's greeting to the Pickwickians, as he met them on the threshold with outstretched arms, and it is in this homely capacity that the dear "old" fellow is seen to best advantage. How he infused his jovial personality into all his guests! Look at the round game they played on the evening of their arrival. Most of the company joined in it, although Mr. Pickwick made one of four with old Mrs. Wardle, for a game of whist, which they played "with all that gravity of deportment and sedateness of demeanour which befit the pursuit."

The round game was Pope Joan, and "so boisterously merry as materially to interrupt the contemplations" of at least one of the whist players. The game is seldom played nowadays, and Pope Joan boards are rareties confined to museums. The game, when played without a board, is similar to "Newmarket." Here is a description of it as played at Mr. Wardle's.

The round game proceeded right merrily. Isabella Wardle and Mr. Trundle "went partners," and Emily Wardle and Mr. Snodgrass did the same; and even Mr. Tupman and the spinster aunt established a joint-stock company of fish and flattery. Old Mr. Wardle was in the very height of his jollity; and he was *so* funny in his management of the board, and the old ladies were *so* sharp after their winnings, that the whole table was in a perpetual roar of merriment and laughter. There was one old lady who always had about half a dozen cards to pay for, at which everybody laughed, regularly every round; and when the old lady looked cross at having to pay, they laughed louder than ever; on which the old lady's face gradually brightened up, till at last she laughed louder than any of them. Then, when the spinster aunt got "matrimony," the young ladies laughed afresh, and the spinster aunt seemed disposed to be pettish; till, feeling Mr. Tupman squeezing her hand under the table, *she* brightened up too, and looked rather knowing as if matrimony in reality were not quite so far off as some people thought for; whereupon everybody laughed again, and especially old Mr. Wardle, who enjoyed a joke as much as the youngest.

5

The Fat Boy, the Cricket Match, and the elopement of Jingle with the Spinster Aunt are all part of the Wardle scenes, and will doubtless be adequately dealt with by other contributors to this centenary volume; but the incidents following the discovery of the latter show Mr. Wardle in an entirely new light. From the complacent yeoman-proprietor of Manor Farm he is converted into a man of action. Mr. Pickwick showed himself to be quite helpless when he heard the news, and lamely asked, "What shall we do?" "Do?" echoed old Wardle. "Put a horse in the gig. I'll get a chaise at the Lion and follow 'em instantly." Mr. Pickwick, never a man of action, could not understand that impulse in others. In an endeavour to restrain the impetuosity of Mr. Wardle he performed the seemingly impossible feat of firmly clasping his arms "round the extensive waist of their corpulent host." But to no avail. In vain did Mr. Wardle demand to be allowed "to get at" the poor Fat Boy, whom he wrongly accused of having been bribed by Jingle. The ladies begged that he be not allowed to go in chase, and in the end Mr. Pickwick decided to accompany his friend on what he considered to be a mad errand.

We have yet to meet the modern author who can write a description of a motor-car chase as vigorous, as boisterous and as humorous as the one detailed by Dickens in chapter nine, when "fields, trees, and hedges seemed to rush past them with the velocity of a whirlwind, so rapid was the pace at which they tore along." When there were delays in obtaining relays of horses, old Wardle was never daunted :

he laid about him with such hearty good-will, cuffing this man, and pushing that; strapping a buckle here, and taking in a link there, that the chaise was ready in a much shorter time than could reasonably have been expected, under so many difficulties.

And when at length they came almost alongside the eloping couple

Old Mr. Wardle foamed with rage and excitement. He roared out scoundrels and villains by the dozen, clenched his fist and shook it expressively at the object of his indignation; but Mr. Jingle only answered with a contemptuous smile, and replied to his menaces by a shout of triumph, as his horses, answering the increased application of whip and spur, broke into a faster gallop, and left the pursuers behind.

Then came the catastrophe: "a sudden bump, a loud crash —away rolled a wheel and over went the chaise." And although old Wardle went over with it, still his ardour was not abated. It was six miles to the next stage where fresh horses could be hired, and the old fellow not only determined to walk it in the drenching rain, but his enthusiasm infected Mr. Pickwick to a similar course. The pursuit was successfully accomplished, and the foolish sister removed from the hands of the adventurer Jingle.

6

It is, however, in the pleasing surroundings of domesticity that we see Mr. Wardle at his best. When we join him in the circle round the fire of the best sitting-room at Manor Farm, a "long dark-panelled room with a high chimney-piece, and a capacious chimney, up which you could have driven one of the new patent cabs, wheels and all," the fire is blazing and crackling on the hearth, and merry voices resound; indeed, "if any of the old English yeomen had turned into fairies when they died, it was just the place in which they would have held their revels." The spirit of all the Wardles that ever were surrounds us, and in an interval of silence the living embodiment of all of them is heard to say, "This is just what I like—the happiest moments of my life have been passed at this old fireside; and I am so attached to it, that I keep up a blazing fire here every evening until it actually grows too hot to bear it."

That was typical of old Wardle; he was always "keeping up" something. We learn later how he kept Christmas, not aloof and alone, but among his servants in the kitchen. "Master wouldn't neglect to keep it up, on any account," said Emma the maid, which brought the glad retort from Sam Weller, "Your master's a wery pretty notion of keepin' up; I never see such a sensible sort of man as he is, or such a reg'lar gen'l'm'n." It was "according to annual custom on Christmas Eve, observed by old Wardle's fore-bears from time immemorial."

From the centre of the ceiling of this kitchen, old Wardle had just suspended with his own hands a huge branch of mistletoe, and the same branch of mistletoe instantaneously gave rise to a scene of general and most delightful struggling and confusion; in the midst of which Mr. Pickwick, with a gallantry which would have done honour to a descendant of Lady Tollimglower herself, took the old lady by the hand, led her beneath the mystic branch, and saluted her in all courtesy and decorum. The old lady submitted to this piece of practical politeness with all the dignity which be-fitted so important and serious a solemnity, but the younger ladies, not being so thoroughly imbued with a superstitious veneration of the custom, or imagining that the value of a salute is very much enhanced if it cost a little trouble to obtain it, screamed and struggled, and ran into corners, and threatened and remonstrated, and did every thing but leave the room, until some of the less adventurous gentlemen were on the point of desisting, when they all at once found it useless to resist any longer, and submitted to be kissed with a good grace. . . .

As to the poor relations, they kissed everybody, not even excepting the plainer portion of the young-lady visitors, who, in their excessive confusion, ran right under the mistletoe, directly it was hung up, without knowing it! Wardle stood with his back to the fire surveying the whole scene, with the utmost satisfaction; and the fat boy took the opportunity of appropriating to his own use, and summarily devouring, a particularly fine mincepie, that had been carefully put by, for somebody else. . . .

When they were all tired of blind-man's buff, there was a great game at snap-dragon, and when fingers enough were burned with that, and all the raisins gone, they sat down by the huge fire of blazing logs to a substantial supper, and a mighty bowl of wassail, something smaller than an ordinary wash-house copper, in which the hot apples were hissing and bubbling with a rich look, and a jolly sound, that were perfectly irresistible.

"This," said Mr. Pickwick, looking round him, "this is, indeed, comfort."

"Our invariable custom," replied Mr. Wardle. "Everybody sits down with us on Christmas eve, as you see them now—servants and all; and here we wait till the clock strikes twelve, to usher Christmas in, and while away the time with forfeits and old stories. Trundle, my boy, rake up the fire."

Up flew the bright sparks in myriads as the logs were stirred, and the deep red blaze sent forth a rich glow, that penetrated into the furthest corner of the room, and cast its cheerful tint on every face.

"Come," said Wardle, "a song—a Christmas song. I'll give you one, in default of a better."

"Bravo," said Mr. Pickwick.

"Fill up," cried Wardle. "It will be two hours good, before you see the bottom of the bowl through the deep rich colour of the wassail; fill up all round, and now for the song."

Mr. Wardle, a "very old gentleman" this time, then sings in a good round sturdy voice "A Christmas Carol" to "the king of the seasons all."

One verse we quote as typifying the season of goodwill and good cheer which Dickens all his life did so much to foster, and of which this chapter of *The Pickwick Papers* is the outstanding example; and you can follow it up for yourselves by reading the story of the goblins who stole a sexton with which the jovial host followed his song; the story that was the forerunner of the real *Christmas Carol*, the most famous story Dickens ever wrote, which has cheered the hearts of countless millions the whole world over; a blessing for which we must thank Mr. Wardle.

> "But my song I troll out, for Christmas stout,
>   The hearty, the true, and the bold;
>   A bumper I drain, and with might and main
>   Give three cheers for this Christmas old.
>   We'll usher him in with a merry din
>   That shall gladden his joyous heart,
>   And we'll keep him up, while there's bite or sup,
>   And in fellowship good, we'll part."

MRS BARDELL

By Beatrice Kean Seymour

IX

ITH most of Dickens's characters we know from the moment of their appearance where we are. They spring into being fully grown, even over-grown, and they do not change or develop. They live statically, as Mr. Chesterton has observed, "in a perpetual summer of being themselves. It was not the aim of Dickens to show the effect of time and circumstances upon a character."

But in Mrs. Bardell we have a character who does not seem to me to fit very neatly into this generalisation. For Mrs. Bardell does develop—if only for the worse. And if the effect of time is not noticeable in regard to her, that of circumstances, I think, certainly is.

What Dickens had to say about her, in the rôle of God Almighty author who is presumed to know everything about his characters, was simply stated. She was introduced to us as Pickwick's landlady—the relict and sole executrix of a deceased custom-house officer. She was a woman of agreeable appearance and bustling manners. She had one child, a boy named Tommy, one other lodger beside Mr. Pickwick, and a natural genius for cooking. Her house in Goswell Street was clean and quiet, and in it "Mr. Pickwick's will was law."

In the first moment of our introduction to her we are able, of our own observation, to add another to these traits—that of feminine curiosity, for as she is engaged in the legitimate business of dusting Mr. Pickwick's apartments, she becomes aware that something of importance

Mrs Bardell faints in Mr Pickwick's arms.

is afoot, and prolongs the flicking of the dust from one place to another in the hope of discovering what is causing Mr. Pickwick to behave so oddly. He had sent her small boy on an errand to the Borough, and now occupied himself in running to and from the window, popping his head in and out and constantly looking at his watch. Mrs. Bardell, who knew that Mr. Pickwick had a well-regulated mind, was undoubtedly and very naturally intrigued by these antics. When he complained that her little boy was a long while gone, she pointed out that the distance from Goswell Street to the Borough was considerable, with which reasonable observation Mr. Pickwick amiably agreed before plunging to his doom.

It is at this point that we begin to suspect that the bustling and efficient Mrs. Bardell may not be all that Dickens's brief introduction has led us to suppose—or, rather, that she may be considerably more. Certainly Mr. Pickwick has not proceeded very far along the road that ends in the abyss before we are faced with a pretty problem. Is Mrs. Bardell a designing woman who has already had her eye on her lodger as a likely fulfiller of the rôle of husband Number Two, or is she just a silly woman who thought that because a man liked her cooking he must be half-way at least in love with her? Did she purposely misunderstand Mr. Pickwick's subsequent remarks or did she, supposing her stupid and her head full of matrimony, genuinely misunderstand them? It is true that up to a point Mr. Pickwick "asked for it," for if in that fateful conversation he was under the impression that he was announcing his intention of keeping a man-servant, it is impossible to resist the conclusion that he made rather a mess of it. Every single remark he permitted himself could as well have been made in reference to a life-partner as to a man-servant. Did Mrs. Bardell think, forsooth, that it was a much greater expense to keep two people than one? "La, Mr. Pickwick," said the lady, blushing and simpering, but Pickwick is not warned. "Well, but *do* you?" he inquires, rushing on his fate. True, our hero is as much the victim of what Mr. Chesterton calls the "queer innocence of the afternoon of life" as he was of Mrs. Bardell's amatory designs or embarrassing folly, but certainly he lets her get very far along the wrong road before he even begins to suspect that all is not well in the State of Denmark. And by then it is too late—Mrs. Bardell has thrown herself into his arms, footsteps are heard ascending the stairs, the door is thrown open, and Mr. Pickwick is discovered "in an extremely awkward situation."

Now what, if anything, is there to say in extenuation of Mrs. Bardell's conduct up to this point? First of all, there is the little fact which Dickens omits to mention until the middle of this unfortunate scene, when Mrs. Bardell is already well away down the wrong road—she "had long worshipped Mr. Pickwick at a distance." So now, "raised to a pinnacle to which her wildest and most extravagant hopes had never dared to aspire," the poor lady is not so much on the wrong road as, like Buckingham in even more embarrassing circumstances, half way to heaven. Living in an age when matrimony so filled the feminine horizon that it is a wonder women ever saw anything else whatsoever upon it, it is quite possible that when on that bright July morning Mrs. Bardell looked at her lodger she saw only an elderly and somewhat agitated old gentleman with something very plainly on his mind. And what, pray, could Mr. Pickwick have to be agitated about, and what could he possibly have upon his mind? Mrs. Bardell's answer to both questions was undoubtedly altogether too hastily arrived at. Had he not already complained that Tommy had been long upon his errand, and what could that mean except that Mr. Pickwick was afraid he might return before he, Mr. Pickwick, had found words suitably to inform Tommy's mother of that for which Tommy had been temporarily banished from the scene? Mr. Pickwick, in short, was about to declare himself—a social occasion which, in those days, as we know, was one calling for considerable tact, sensibility and that very circumlocution of speech in which the poor gentleman was only too palpably indulging. Mr. Pickwick, in an ecstasy of trepidation lest Sammy Weller should not be found, or, being found, should fail to answer the summons; Mr. Pickwick, behaving like an excited child at the expectation of a new toy, was only to the bewitched and beglamoured Mrs. Bardell a nervous elderly gentleman finding it vastly difficult to come to the point. Mrs. Bardell, in short, like the rest of us, was only believing what she wanted to believe.

That, I submit, makes her a fool very probably—almost certainly—but it does not make her a knave, else are we all undone. Was she ever that, and if so at what point did her metamorphosis begin?

We are not told what happened to Mrs. Bardell that morning after Mr. Pickwick, with the assistance of Tommy, had conducted her downstairs, for Dickens shifts our interest at once to Pickwick's lively interview and subsequent shopping expedition with the redoubtable Sammy. But we do know that Mrs. Cluppins was in the house at the time, having, as she later told the little judge, looked in to say good morning "in a promiscuous

manner," at that very moment when Pickwick was com-
bining entreaty with remonstrance, to such poor purpose,
to the half-fainting lady in his arms. Presumably then
(unless Mrs. Cluppins was perjuring herself) at the time
Mr. Pickwick was conducting his interview with Sammy
in his sitting-room on the first floor, Mrs. Bardell was un-
burdening her heart to Mrs. Cluppins. But of what? Did
she allege then that Mr. Pickwick had declared himself?
That she was the happiest woman alive? We must suppose
so, since, at the trial, that other sympathetic female, Mrs.
Sanders, assured the Court that the current topic of conversation in the neighbourhood, "after the fainting in
July," was Mrs. Bardell's engagement to Mr. Pickwick—
or was that loquacious lady also committing perjury? At
what point, then, between that sunny morning in July
and the end of August, when Mr. Pickwick's holiday in
the country was disturbed by the sinister threat of a Writ
for Breach of Promise, did Mrs. Bardell begin to perceive
that she had made a most dreadful mistake? Or did she
never perceive that but only that Mr. Pickwick had
changed his mind? That, we must suppose, would have
been obvious almost at once, since Mrs. Bardell was still
the landlady and Mr. Pickwick still in residence and still,
presumably, in need of her good meals. But these facts
remain—that the very next morning Mr. Pickwick took
his seat with his friends inside the Eatanswill coach (upon
the outside of which Sammy Weller swung himself,
resplendent in new grey coat, black cockaded hat, and pink
striped waistcoat) without any sign of the trepidation
which one would expect after a painful interview with a
lady who considered that her feelings had been trifled with.
Moreover, when Mr. Pickwick receives the letter from

Dodson and Fogg acquainting him with the fact that Mrs. Bardell had "commenced an action," he is completely taken by surprise; more, he asserts on the instant that it was a "base conspiracy between two sets of grasping attorneys," and that "Mrs. Bardell would never do it— she hasn't the heart to do it—she hasn't the case to do it."

At what point then did Mrs. Bardell discover that she had? More properly, perhaps, at what point did those amiable ladies, Mrs. Cluppins and Mrs. Sanders, begin to make clear to her what her duty was to herself, her son, and her sex? When did those "grasping attorneys" first make their appearance upon the scene? And at whose instigation? Let us remember Sammy Weller's subsequent dark hints as to those "kind and generous people as sets their clerks to work to find out little disputes among their neighbours and acquaintances as vants settlin' by means o' law suits." Let us not forget, either, Mr. Pickwick's surprise and his instant repudiation of his landlady's share in the business. Giving Mrs. Bardell, therefore, the benefit of the doubt, I submit she was "got at." The first stage of her metamorphosis had begun.

Was she ever really the vengeful litigant determined to humiliate the man she had so recently "worshipped at a distance"? I doubt it, but since man, in his inscrutable wisdom, had learnt to measure injured feelings and broken hearts in terms of £ *s. d.* it was but natural that the Dodsons and Foggs should make their appearance upon the earthly scene and obvious that such people as Mrs. Bardell were exactly what they were looking for. So, gradually, the bustling housewife becomes the lorn and helpless female, the innocent victim of the wiles of that monster, the lordly male; and, presently, the wronged and piteous heroine of melodrama. Even Mrs. Bardell, I think, must have been a little surprised at what those clever lawyers, and later, the exuberant Serjeant Buzfuz, made of her between them.

Take a look at her soon after her initiation. The Writ has been served and Mr. Pickwick sends Sam Weller to collect his belongings from Goswell Street and to adjust the little matter of the rent. Also, with a view to discovering what he can as to the lie of the land, the state of Mrs. Bardell's mind towards him, and whether or no this "vile and groundless action" is to go forward. On being admitted by that hinfant fernomenon, Tommy Bardell, Sam finds that young gentleman's mother in the company of that precious pair, Mrs. Elizabeth Cluppins and Mrs. Susannah Sanders. Buttressed as she was by their tender sympathy and moral support, she yet "felt it proper to be agitated," and turned pale. She weeps a little, pays a handsome compliment to Sam's master and offers Sam a little "something to keep out the cold," but is still sufficiently agitated to fill three glasses instead of one—to the entire satisfaction of Messrs. Cluppins and Sanders. Surely, however, it was Mrs. Bardell, the fool, not Mrs. Bardell the student of those "grasping attorneys," Messrs. Dodson and Fogg, who informed Sam that "she supposed he knew what was going forward," acquainted him with their opinion that, "with the evidence as we shall call we must succeed," did nothing to contradict his outrageous implication regarding "them Dodson and Fogg as does these sort of things on spec," and took all his heavy irony with perfect seriousness? Like all other people engaged in playing a part, there were times when Mrs. Bardell forgot her lines and substituted others that must have been a little disconcerting to her coachers and backers.

Nevertheless, when the case comes for trial it is obvious that Messrs. Dodson and Fogg have done their work with no small measure of success. She has obviously been submitted to a rigid course of coaching, and doubtless by now she has come to believe that Pickwick has really done her an injury which can only be wiped out by the payment of a large sum of money—a very human conclusion, after all. Certainly her entry into court is a triumph—for Messrs. Dodson and Fogg as well as for Dickens. It was excellently timed, breaking in upon Pickwick's horrified contemplation of the juror who had just sat down after explaining to the Judge that owing to the Crown's insistence upon his presence his chemist's shop had been left in charge of an errand boy who laboured under the impression that Epsom salts meant oxalic acid and senna extract laudanum! Complete with umbrella, pattens, and drooping mien, the plaintiff is deposited at the far end of the same bench upon which Pickwick is seated, the faithful Cluppins at her side. Enter Mrs. Sanders, with Tommy, when Mrs. Bardell goes all maternal, clutches the boy to her bosom, becomes hysterical, and finally requests piteously to be told where she is. Those clever lawyers, Messrs. Dodson and Fogg, implore her to compose herself, Serjeant Buzfuz rubs his eyes with his white handkerchief and the judge is visibly affected. Excellent. Mrs. Bardell has played up; done all—and more than all—that was expected of her. Mrs. Bardell, in short, has made an exhibition of herself. The rest is with Buzfuz.

Buzfuz knows his job and proceeds to it with dispatch. In his hands the character of Mrs. Bardell "swells wisibly," assisted by a finely imaginative preluding effort in respect of the late Mr. Bardell. This gentleman we learn, having enjoyed for years the esteem and confidence of his sovereign "glided almost imperceptibly from the world" —a Buzfuzzian euphemism for the prosaic fact that he was knocked on the head with a quart pot in the cellar of a public-house—but not before he had "stamped his likeness upon a little boy," the hinfant fernomenon to wit, one Tommy. With this young gentleman, as "the only pledge of her departed exciseman," Mrs. Bardell has repaired to Goswell Street and taken to letting lodgings for single gentlemen. Why *single* gentlemen? Because Mrs. Bardell has no fear of single gentlemen, no distrust, no suspicion; on the contrary, it is in single gentlemen that she now reposes her whole trust, for she remembers that Mr. Bardell, in addition to being a man of honour, of his word, and no deceiver, was himself once a single gentleman. For years, shrinking from the world in the retirement and tranquillity of Goswell Street, Mrs. Bardell has ministered to the creature comforts of such single gentlemen as "inquired within" and took her lodgings; in particular, to those of that single gentleman against whom she has now most cruelly been forced to bring this action. Not only did she cook his meals, look after his washing, darn, air, and prepare it for wear, but she enjoyed his fullest confidence. With much dark talk of chops and tomato sauce, of delayed returns from journeys from home, of slow coaches and warming-pans, does the impassioned Buzfuz draw a horrifying picture of a sensitive and confiding female, a lonely and desolate widow, whose hopes and prospects have been ruined, whose occupation (not to say pre-occupation) with single gentlemen has gone for ever, filched from her by that despicable wretch and inhuman monster, Pickwick. Never, in short, in the whole of his professional experience had Serjeant Buzfuz approached a case with feelings of such deep emotion. . . . Did Mrs. Bardell blush? Did she feel that it would be a mercy if Mrs. Cluppins would actually open the umbrella with which she had for so long been fidgeting, so that she might hide herself behind it? Or was she past blushes, past thought, past everything, save the gloating contemplation of those heavy damages for which she had allowed herself to be dragged "in this terrible fashion before the public"? Dickens doesn't tell us, and, to be frank, I am sure he didn't care. He had long ago taken leave of the Mrs. Bardell to whom, at the beginning of Chapter Seven, he so neatly introduced us and is now concerned only with the fantastic, highly-coloured lady Serjeant Buzfuz is presenting to the twelve good men and true, and who would scarcely be taken for her first cousin. That gentleman, certainly, nearly falls into an apoplexy in his efforts to get all the high lights possible into his portrait, so that we, too, temporarily forget Mrs. Bardell and remember suddenly something which Mr. Chesterton says of another of Dickens's characters—the unforgettable Mr. Guppy. Perhaps, he says, we *could* have created Mr. Guppy, but the effort would have so exhausted us that for ever afterwards we should have been wheeled about in a bath-chair. Serjeant Buzfuz, showing no sign of exhaustion, no immediate need of the bath-chair, with his face very red and his composure only most temporarily ruffled at the hands of the redoubtable Sammy, stands there in Court and in time as the only true begetter of Martha Bardell. He had every reason to feel proud of his performance.

Yet that poor deluded creature is not without real pathos, for she, too, was a victim of those same nits of the

law in whose toils Mr. Pickwick had been so easily entangled. For those "grasping attorneys," Messrs. Dodson
and Fogg, having dragged her through the Courts for
their own profit, took the precaution to get her signature
to a deed under which, when later Pickwick refused on
principle to pay their costs, they speedily consigned her to
the horrors of the Debtors' Prison in the Fleet. And her
last appearance, when Dodson and Fogg and Buzfuz have
done their damnedest with her is a humble one enough;
for does she not express, by proxy, her deep regret at
having been the instrument of annoyance or injury to
Mr. Pickwick and earnestly implore his pardon?

Nevertheless, although as the simple human being to
whom Dickens first introduces us, she is at once the least
extraordinary and least exaggerated of his minor characters, she does become, in the hands first of Dodson and
Fogg and subsequently of the egregious Buzfuz, a figure
of genuine comedy.

What we laugh at in Mrs. Bardell, what the man in the
street laughed at upon her first appearance in the *Papers*,
is not what she was but what was made of her. She stands
as an eternal example of what can be done with the most
simple and unlikely material by those clever enough and
unscrupulous enough to exploit it. She is the prototype of
every silly woman who has ever sought to reduce affection
to a monetary basis, who, if she cannot have a man's name
and a share of his bed and board, is determined at least to
have some part of his cash.

The ultimate truth, of course, is that Mrs. Bardell is not
in *Pickwick*, as is Mrs. Leo Hunter, for the mere purpose of
"being a character." Neither, except in the very limited
sense of poor Pickwick, is she put there, as are Dickens's

villains, to be a menace and a danger to the innocent-minded. She was conceived as a piece of machinery, and from first to last that is what she is—a piece of machinery most cunningly devised and manipulated. Through her Dickens was able, under cover of writing an amusing and riotously ridiculous incident, to satirise a stupid law and those who turned it to their own account, trading on human folly and cupidity. Nobody but Dickens, I think, could have succeeded so well in this intention and contrived, at the same time, to do so much more. For whatever he meant in the first place to do with poor Martha Bardell, it is certain that he ended by giving us a portrait which, if smaller, is by no means unworthy to take its place among those others which, for all Dickensians, must hang for ever on the wall of Memory.

SERGEANT BUZFUZ
By Bernard Darwin

X

"SEVEN hundred and fifty pounds," said the foreman of the jury: The Court rose. Mr. Justice Stareleigh bobbed and waddled out and Sergeant Buzfuz, rubbing his hands, turned with a smile to his junior. He had been a little sharp with him once or twice in the heat of the conflict, but now he radiated affability.

"A most satisfactory verdict," he said, "and by no means unfortunate. I hardly think our friend Snubbin was quite—eh, my dear Skimpin? But we must not be censorious, we all make our mistakes. And by the way that was an excellent point of yours with that fellow Winkle. How was it you turned his words?—Compose yourself to this situation. Capital, capital—I never heard anything better done. I am sure I am much obliged to you."

Mr. Skimpin accepted his leader's praise with becoming modesty, but let us listen to him later in his own chambers when holding forth on the case to his reverential pupil. Then he was sufficiently outspoken.

"We had scarcely the ghost of a case," he said. "I was trembling lest we should be non-suited, and what a time I had with old Buzfuz! He would put both feet right into it. I couldn't stop him with that witness Weller. Of course you saw me trying, didn't you? But once he gets the bit between his teeth there's no holding him."

The pupil had observed and was suitably sympathetic, but ventured to think that the Sergeant's speech had been rather effective.

The Trial.

"Oh yes," admitted Mr. Skimpin, "he can come the bricks and mortar business well enough, I will say. The old impostor! Rubbing his eyes with his handkerchief and looking at the jury—but, of course, what won us the case was the way Snubbin handled it. Look here, my dear fellow, if you want a model of how not to conduct a case you had it to-day. You ought to make a careful note of everything Snubbin did and then avoid it." The pupil certainly had thought some things rather odd. Had not Mr. Skimpin, for example, come near to cross-examining his own witnesses? And why had there been no objection?

"Of course I did," said Mr. Skimpin, "as hard as I could and Snubbin never moved a muscle. I don't know what old Stareleigh was thinking about. Lucky for us he was asleep most of the time. Then he was made peppery to begin with because he got Winkle's name wrong. He's deaf as a post and hates anyone to find it out. And Snubbin didn't cross-examine Mrs. Cluppins. Was there ever such nonsense?—I could have turned her inside out. What on earth was he doing, too, letting Phunky cross-examine Winkle? Why the fellow's never had a brief before in his life, and will never get one again I should think. Well, well, I wish Buzfuz had let me take Weller. He wouldn't have made such a fool of me, I flatter myself. However, he's not a bad old fellow and said some very handsome things to me afterwards."

The pupil anxious to originate something on his own account remarked that that was an interesting point raised by the Judge as to what the soldier said not being evidence. Now if the soldier— Mr. Skimpin cut in again.

"Even he is awake sometimes," he said, "when it doesn't matter, but I suppose you saw that he let in some hearsay evidence another time. I'll give Buzfuz credit for that. When that woman Sanders was in the box he got out of her what all the neighbours said about Mrs. Bardell being engaged. There was a woman who kept a mangle—Mrs. Mudkins——"

"Mrs. Mudberry," exclaimed the pupil proudly, "and Mrs. Bunkin who clear starched."

"Well, their names are of no importance," said Mr. Skimpin crushingly. "The important thing is that what they said was not evidence at all, and yet there was old Snubbin—daren't say bo to a goose. Lord knows how he gets all the work he does," and Mr. Skimpin, flushed with victory, reflected that he had half a mind to ask the Lord Chancellor for a silk gown.

2

We have heard Mr. Skimpin's views and now what are our own? Like other great leaders in history, Mr. Sergeant Buzfuz owes his celebrity in a large measure to the mistakes of his enemies. We must presume that Mr. Perker had some good reason for his assertion that Mr. Sergeant Snubbin led the court by the nose; he may have shone in the case about the stopping up of a pathway leading "from some place which nobody ever came from to some other place which nobody ever went to," but he allowed himself to be utterly out-manœuvred in the rough and tumble of a breach of promise. Why Mr. Phunky was briefed as his junior we have no means of knowing. It can only be inferred that Mr. Perker wanted to please somebody. Perhaps he was a nephew of one of those "very good country agencies" who were dining with the little attorney at Montague Square on the occasion when Job Trotter went there with Sam's message and "got the key of the street."

Messrs. Dodson and Fogg were not likely to be guided by any such benevolent motives, and made no mistake in choosing Mr. Skimpin as Sergeant Buzfuz's junior. Indeed, there are some who share Mr. Skimpin's own opinion: they hold that it is chiefly to him that the glory of victory should belong, since he struck the first telling blow by reducing Mr. Winkle to that state of confusion which ended in his fatal admission as to the affair of Miss Witherfield at Ipswich. It would, however, be rash to accept this view. There has seldom been a successful general, but that we have been told in confidence that he was but the figurehead and that the main credit belonged to his Chief of Staff, and Sergeant Buzfuz undeniably possessed some great qualities. Humour and lightness of touch were not his strong points, and when he tried to make a joke about greasing the wheels of that criminally slow coach, Mr. Pickwick, none of the jurymen understood it except the greengrocer, but he was a master both of pathos and rhetoric. His description of the death of Mr. Bardell was magnificent and will be long remembered as a piece of forensic eloquence. We cannot hear the tone of peculiar richness and volume in which the words were delivered, but even when reduced to cold print they cannot fail to move. Mr. Skimpin was a perky, complacent little upstart of a man. Such a flight was altogether beyond him as was that noble piece of invective which ends "be his name Pickwick or Noakes or Stoakes or Stiles or Brown or Thompson."

It must be remembered, too, that the Sergeant's treatment of one of the weakest and flimsiest parts of his case was taken as a model by a distinguished advocate some years afterwards. As I shall point out later in another connection, it is impossible to say for certain how many years, but it was certainly some. Most people would have seen nothing in Mr. Pickwick's two notes as to chops and tomata sauce and the warming pan, but in the Sergeant's hands they became "far more conclusive than if couched in the most glowing language and the most poetic imagery," while the warming-pan in particular glowed as "a mere cover for hidden fire." In 1835 came the famous action for *crim con, Norton* v. *Melbourne.* There were three notes from Lord Melbourne to Mrs. Norton which were apparently of the most innocent description, but Sir William Follett for the plaintiff declared that they "imparted much more than the mere words conveyed," and that there was "something in the style of them which led at least to something like suspicion." He added "it seems that there may be latent love like latent heat in these productions." There is something in the style of these remarks which leads not to suspicion but to certainty. Sir William had possibly sat as a briefless junior in the Guildhall listening to the Sergeant and now reproduced his words. Ill-gotten goods did not prosper and he lost his case, but he had paid the Sergeant the highest compliment he could.

Sergeant Buzfuz had the defects of his qualities. He had, as we know, a fat body and a red face, and men of this apoplectic habit are apt to be tempestuous at times. The Sergeant did sometimes grow over-excited and was probably at his best in a speech rather than in the examination of witnesses. An indiscretion may escape notice in a torrent of words, but it is otherwise with a question to a witness, and he did sometimes make the infinitely perilous mistake of asking a question without knowing what the answer was going to be. This rashness let him into a sad tangle in his examination of Mr. Weller. He ought to have known that Sam had not been present at the fainting scene in Goswell Street. Mr. Skimpin was pulling at his gown, but he plunged recklessly ahead only to be made ridiculous. Perhaps he could hardly have expected Sam's answer as to Dodson and Fogg taking up the case on spec, and yet he ought to have scented danger. If he had not won the case we may guess that he would never have had another brief from Freeman's Court. On the other hand, he cunningly allowed Mr. Phunky enough rope with which to hang himself in the cross-examination of Mr. Winkle. On the whole we may set him down as a dangerous advocate to his own side as well as to the other, capable of flashes of brilliancy as well as of almost irreparable mistakes.

As regards his private life we have no evidence whatever. We do not even know his Christian name, and if I personally believe it to have been John (he signed himself, as I fancy, "Jno"), others are perfectly at liberty to think of him as Thomas. As a human being I believe him to have been an irritable, hot-headed, but not unkindly man. He was always inclined to be friendly, as witness his pleasant greeting to Sergeant Snubbin before the case began, and bore no malice after the fray was over. If he was unscrupulous in his tactics and something of a bully, such was the fashion of his day at the Bar. No doubt if he had been pressed he would have said, as did a famous Yorkshire jockey, that he had done as many as had done him. He was not a model of sensitiveness or refinement; he had had to

141

thrust and fight his own way through a crowd of competitors; he enjoyed his bottle of port and liked to gobble his turtle soup with his fellow benchers. Do not let us be too hard on him.

3

Now I come, not without trepidation, to what I venture to call a discovery about Sergeant Buzfuz. It may be one on which doubt will be cast, as doubt was impiously cast on that made by Mr. Pickwick outside the house of Mr. W. Stumps at Cobham. Some "presumptuous and ill-conditioned Blotton" who does not cultivate the mysterious and the sublime may possibly declare that I am a humbug. Again I cannot altogether forget that scientific gentleman who lived near Bristol and saw the mysterious lights in the lane. Somebody may say to me, as the scientific gentleman said to his servant on that occasion (his immortal name was Pruffle), "You're a fool and may go downstairs." Such is often the fate of discoverers and must be born with philosophy, more especially as for various reasons which it is impossible to disclose I cannot produce the clear-cut evidence I should like. I offer then my conclusions for what they may be worth, and Pickwickian students can take them or leave them. Let it at least be said for me that my methods are founded on the best models. Those who are acquainted with the unwearied researches of Dickensian scholars know how they can discover certain people in books to be certain other people in real life, though they have, to the careless and superficial eye, no resemblance to them whatever; they can by an uncanny intuition identify a public-house

once called the Peacock for no ostensibly better reason
than that it is now called the Swan. Things come into
their heads that would never come into those of ordinary
mortals, and I have endeavoured, faint and pursuing, to
follow them.

My theory is that Sergeant Buzfuz was a nephew of
another distinguished advocate of a rather earlier day, Mr.
Stryver. Sometimes I have thought, indeed, that if Mr.
Stryver had called him his son instead of his nephew he
would not have been far wrong. No doubt he led a wild
life before he had settled down when he used to carouse
nightly in the Temple with Sydney Carton. However, I
have perhaps no right to say so much; nephew it shall be.
It can hardly be necessary, I hope, to recall the details of
Mr. Stryver's career. Oddly enough, though older by a
number of years than Sergeant Buzfuz, he became known
to the general public considerably later, for by some
curious chance the great case of *Rex* v. *Darnay*, which
made his name, was not reported till twenty-three years
after Bardell and Pickwick (see *Tale of Two Cities*, 1859).

Clearly in order to make anything of my case I must
show that it is at least a possible one in point of time. This
may, I fear, be dull, and it must inevitably be difficult, for
we are at once brought face to face with a chronological
contradiction which has, so far as I know, baffled all
inquirers. As regards Mr. Stryver there is no question.
The case of *Rex* v. *Darnay* was tried at the Old Bailey in
1780. The journey of Mr. Lorry by the Dover Mail, in
which the prisoner was supposed to have been a passenger,
took place in 1775, and Book II, at the beginning of
which the trial is described, is entitled "Five Years Later."
We are expressly told that at the date of the trial Mr.

Stryver was "a man of little more than thirty." Assume him to have been thirty-two and we get the date of his birth as 1748.

The difficulty arises as to Sergeant Buzfuz. Assuming him to have been of much the same age as his opponent Sergeant Snubbin, we may say that he was "about five-and-forty, or he might be fifty." But when was he of that age? That depends on the date of the trial to which there are two schools of thought. One school pins its faith to the Transactions of the Pickwick Club, and it is hard to imagine a higher authority. The first minute recorded is of the historic meeting (with Joseph Smiggers, Esq., P.V.P.M.P.C., presiding) at which the Corresponding Society of the Club was constituted. That minute is dated May 12, 1817, and it is incontestable that immediately after the meeting Mr. Pickwick and his three friends set out on their travels by the Commodore Coach. A minor difficulty arises owing to the fact that at Ipswich the boys had dispersed to cricket, and yet almost immediately afterwards Mr. Pickwick set out for his Christmas visit to Dingley Dell. Owing to this hiatus there are some who refuse to accept it as certain that Bardell and Pickwick was tried on St. Valentine's Day, 1818, but at least it cannot possibly have been later than 1819. And yet, as the second school of thought point out, we are confronted with this staggering fact: the letter from Dodson and Fogg, intimating that a writ had been issued was dated August 28, 1830, and in that case the trial must have taken place on February 14, 1831. I am aware that in the Errata in the first edition of *Pickwick*, an attempt has been made to reconcile these two dates by changing the year in each case to 1827; but I cannot think that any authority however high can presume to override the Transactions of the Pickwick Club.

By good fortune my theory is not vitally affected whichever school is right. If Bardell and Pickwick was tried in 1818, and Sergeant Buzfuz was fifty at the time, he must have been born in 1768. That is to say he was born when Mr. Stryver was no more than twenty years old, which makes improbable the more scandalous supposition as to the relationship between them. On the other hand, if the trial was in 1831, Sergeant Buzfuz was born in 1781, when Mr. Stryver was thirty-three and was not yet married. In the latter case Mr. Stryver would have been only in the comparatively early fifties when Mr. Sergeant Buzfuz was eating his dinner and being called to the Bar. It is probable though not certain that Mr. Stryver ultimately reached the Bench, since we are told that about 1792 he was "far on his way to State promotion." If this were so he would have the greater ability to help his young protégé on his road. He had three step-sons, having married "a florid widow with property and three boys," but these boys are described as having "nothing particularly shining about them but the straight hair of their dumpling heads." It would clearly be a mistake to send boys so commonplace and unpromising to the Bar. It is likely that they were put into some safe and pedestrian line of business, where their mother's money could perhaps buy them a small partnership. Any patronage which Mr. Stryver could give would therefore be at the disposal of his nephew Buzfuz, whom I am inclined to believe he had sent to his old school Shrewsbury.

It may be urged that these considerations would apply equally to any barrister of the same age as Sergeant Buzfuz, but I think that it will scarcely be denied that there was a strong family likeness between him and Mr. Stryver which I personally look upon as much more than a coincidence. Buzfuz, as we have already seen, had a fat body and a red face; Stryver was "stout, loud, red, and bluff"; I entreat the attention of the jury of my readers to those words. Again, in another passage, we are told that he was florid and "like a great sunflower," so that to Mr. Lorry's eye there appeared "so much too much of him." He had a Buzfuzian habit of shouldering himself through a crowd and into any company; he was, we hear, for ever "driving, riving, shouldering, pressing." He made himself agreeable on principle, and so did Sergeant Buzfuz when he told Sergeant Snubbin that it was a fine morning. Finally, as regards his advocacy, he was "a glib man and an unscrupulous, and a ready, and a bold," but he badly needed the help of a competent devil or "jackal" in Sydney Carton, and we have to admit that Sergeant Buzfuz would have done all the better to pay more attention to Mr. Skimpin.

As far as we can compare their methods of advocacy it would seem that, while there is a certain likeness, Mr. Stryver was less given to the violent and the spectacular than was the Sergeant. His speech in *Rex* v. *Darnay* was in the nature of a persuasive argument and an appeal to reason rather than to emotion. At the same time he was capable of an outburst at the right moment as shown by his words about "the vile and infamous character of evidence of which the State Trials of this country were full." He was an excellent cross-examiner, a better one as far as we can judge than Buzfuz, but it must be remembered he had admirable material for the demolition of Barsad and Cly; in short he had a good case and Sergeant

146

Buzfuz had an extremely shaky one. It would be pushing my point too far to lay much stress on resemblance of method in two very different cases.

Whichever was the better advocate I have no doubt which was the pleasanter man. There is really nothing to be said for Mr. Stryver; he was wholly intolerable, but there was, I am sure, a spark of kindliness about the Sergeant. Indeed, it is my private belief that once, years after the trial, when they were both growing old, he met Mr. Pickwick on a walk near Dulwich and would have liked to speak to him. Sam was in attendance and the Sergeant recognised his old adversary with a smile, but Mr. Pickwick walked straight by with a set mouth and glittering spectacles, and Sam could only give a surreptitious wink as he passed.

MESSRS DODSON AND FOGG

By E. S. P. Haynes

XI

MESSRS. DODSON AND FOGG have always been figures of fun for anyone who wishes to throw stones at my profession, and when I was asked to write about them I wrote to a legal friend who is more concerned with litigation in the King's Bench Division than I am. He writes to me as follows: "My feeling is that Dickens did an injustice to Dodson and Fogg. They heard, probably from a friend of their Managing Clerk, that Mrs. Bardell had been very shabbily treated, and Mrs. Bardell, if she had, as she probably had, long had hopes of Mr. Pickwick falling for her, was so disappointed that she thoroughly believed that she had been shabbily treated.   Messrs. Dodson and Fogg generously undertook the case and risked a good deal, because Serjeant Buzfuz was extremely unlikely to have gone into court without having been paid the fee on his brief. Messrs. Dodson and Fogg were justified because after all, Mrs. Bardell got judgment. Messrs. Dodson and Fogg were legally entitled to go to her for costs as between solicitor and own client, and I know of no legal reform which has prevented attorneys from doing the same. It may be that the establishment of the Law Society and the disciplinary powers conferred on it may have caused attorneys to think twice before taking litigation on spec, but you and I know that any legal reform of that nature has been entirely inefficacious.

"I recently defended a claim for damages for wrongful imprisonment. Plaintiff was charged by my clients with

Mr. Pickwick & Sam, in the attorneys office.

having taken goods from the counter in their chain stores. Through a misunderstanding with the police, my clients' witness-employee did not turn up at the proper time, and the man was discharged. He somehow got into touch with a lady solicitor, who brought the action, and at the trial, which cost my clients about £60, he admitted having had about ten previous convictions for shoplifting. He was, of course, entirely without means. There is quite a lot to be said for Messrs. Dodson and Fogg, because if they had never existed, many a poor man with a good case would have been left entirely without redress. 'Poor person' procedure is a new thing. Then, although you may not have been afflicted with as much litigation as I have endured, you have, I imagine, had your fair share of trouble with Moneylenders' Solicitors."

I sympathise with his view that a solicitor who undertakes an action on its merits without demanding costs on account is often the only resource of a poor litigant, and even the present admirable system of the Poor Man's Lawyer leaves out many deserving cases just above the margin of relief. The right of a solicitor to take an action on speculative terms has been vindicated as recently as 1928 in *Wiggins* v. *Lavy*.

On the other hand, he does not tackle the main point against Messrs. Dodson and Fogg, which is that having promised to take the action at their own risk they made Mrs. Bardell swear a document known as a *cognovit actionem*, which she probably signed without having the least idea that it would operate as a judgment. In fact this abuse was specially dealt with by an Act of 1838, under which Mrs. Bardell could not have executed the document except in the presence of another attorney who would have explained to her what she was doing. This was probably in Dickens's mind when in a later preface he wrote "Legal reforms have pared the claws of Messrs. Dodson and Fogg" and incidentally it is interesting to note the compliments which he pays to solicitors' clerks for "a spirit of self-respect, mutual forbearance, education, and co-operation for good ends."

I should perhaps also direct the attention of my readers to a most admirably witty and plausible vindication of Dodson and Fogg in Mr. E. V. B. Christian's *Leaves of the Lower Branch*. Incidentally he casts some slur on Pickwick for not calling as witness for the defence the baker who he conjectured would shortly be marrying Mrs. Bardell at the time of the unhappy interview with her. He also points out that Mr. Perker advised "throwing dust in the eyes of the judge."

It is clear, however, that Dickens had a prejudice in favour of solicitors who practised in the Chancery Division as opposed to attorneys who practised in the King's Bench Division, although at the time of *Bardell* v. *Pickwick* most practitioners were both attorneys and solicitors. Mr. Perker, a solicitor, whose work was more in the Chancery Division, briefed a Chancery counsel. Serjeant Snubbin was obviously intended to be a gentleman, although rather too gentlemanly for the purpose of saving Pickwick from the wiles of Messrs. Dodson and Fogg and Serjeant Buzfuz. Throughout the book Perker invariably shows considerable tact and good feeling although he must have considerably annoyed Mr. Pickwick by his persistent praise of Messrs. Dodson and Fogg as sharp lawyers.

Messrs. Dodson and Fogg are certainly made most unattractive. Fogg "was an elderly, pimply-faced, vegetable diet sort of man, in a black coat, dark mixture trousers, and small black gaiters; a kind of being who seemed to be an essential part of the desk at which he was writing, and to have as much thought or sentiment." Dodson was "a plump, portly, stern looking man with a loud voice."

The incidents reported in their office are most unpleasing and I imagine that if Mrs. Bardell, after leaving the Fleet had been able or inclined to employ other lawyers who assisted poor clients, she might have made them very uncomfortable by appealing to the Master of the Rolls with a view to striking them off the Rolls. She could have made a complaint either to the old Society of Gentlemen Practisers or to the Master of the Rolls direct. In one respect, however, Messrs. Dodson and Fogg set an admirable example to other solicitors, namely, that they preserved a most perfect harmony in partnership. One would imagine from the proceedings of Messrs. Dodson and Fogg that they were inseparable, for one of them hardly ever appears without the other. Indeed, but for the frequent mention of their large practice one might have supposed that they had not too much to do. One can only infer that there was such a strong affection between them that they found it impossible to do business unless they were together for the purpose. For this shining example of concord in business they have never perhaps received due commendation, and it is noticeable that other lawyers mentioned by Dickens do not so obviously display the amiable qualities of Messrs. Dodson and Fogg as partners.

Their collaboration (with Dodson as orator and Fogg as subordinate speaker) is well illustrated by their joint interview with Pickwick and Sam Weller, for Fogg refuses to talk without Dodson, who is promptly summoned to Fogg's room:

"Very well, gentlemen, very well," said Mr. Pickwick, rising in person and wrath at the same time; "you shall hear from my solicitor, gentlemen."

"We shall be very happy to do so," said Fogg, rubbing his hands.

"Very," said Dodson, opening the door.

"And before I go, gentlemen," said the excited Mr. Pickwick turning round on the landing, "permit me to say, that of all the disgraceful and rascally proceedings——"

"Stay, sir, stay," interposed Dodson with great politeness. "Mr. Jackson! Mr. Wicks."

"Sir," said the two clerks, appearing at the bottom of the stairs.

"I merely want you to hear what this gentleman says," replied Dodson. "Pray go on, sir—disgraceful and rascally proceedings, I think you said."

"I did," said Mr. Pickwick, thoroughly roused. "I said, sir, that of all the disgraceful and rascally proceedings that ever were attempted, this is the most so. I repeat it, sir."

"You hear that, Mr. Wicks?" said Dodson.

"You won't forget these expressions, Mr. Jackson?" said Fogg.

"Perhaps you would like to call us swindlers, sir," said Dodson. "Pray do, sir, if you feel disposed; now pray do, sir."

"I do," said Mr. Pickwick. "You are swindlers."

"Very good," said Dodson. "You can hear down there, I hope, Mr. Wicks?"

"Oh yes, sir," said Wicks.

"You had better come up a step or two higher, if you can't," added Mr. Fogg. "Go on, sir; do go on. You had better call us thieves, sir; or perhaps you would like to assault one of us. Pray do it, sir, if you would; we will not make the smallest resistance. Pray do it, sir."

As Fogg put himself very temptingly within the reach of Mr. Pickwick's clenched fist, there is little doubt that that gentleman would have complied with his earnest entreaty, but for the interposition of Sam, who, hearing the dispute, emerged from the office, mounted the stairs, and seized his master by the arm.

"You just come away," said Mr. Weller. "Battledore and shuttlecock's a wery good game, vhen you an't the shuttlecock and two lawyers the battledores, in which case it gets too excitin' to be pleasant. Come away, sir. If you want to ease your mind by blowing up somebody, come out into the court and blow me up; but it's rayther too expensive work to be carried on here."

A similar interview takes place when Pickwick pays the costs of the breach of promise action.

"I am very happy," said Fogg, softened by the cheque, "to have had the pleasure of making Mr. Pickwick's acquaintance. I hope you don't think quite so ill of us, Mr. Pickwick, as when we first had the pleasure of seeing you."

"I hope not," said Dodson, with the high tone of calumniated virtue. "Mr. Pickwick now knows us better, I trust; whatever your opinion of gentlemen of our profession may be, I beg to assure you, sir, that I bear no ill-will or vindictive feeling towards you for the sentiments you thought proper to express in our office in Freeman's Court, Cornhill, on the occasion to which my partner has referred."

"Oh no, no; nor I," said Fogg, in a most forgiving manner.

"Our conduct, sir," said Dodson, "will speak for itself, and justify itself, I hope, upon every occasion. We have been in the profession some years, Mr. Pickwick, and have been honoured with the confidence of many excellent clients. I wish you good morning, sir."

"Good morning, Mr. Pickwick," said Fogg. So saying, he put his umbrella under his arm, drew off his right glove, and extended the hand of reconciliation to that most indignant gentleman, who, thereupon, thrust his hands beneath his coat tails, and eyed the attorney with looks of scornful amazement.

"Lowten!" cried Perker at this moment. "Open the door."

"Wait one instant," said Mr. Pickwick, "Perker, I will speak."

"My dear sir, pray let the matter rest where it is," said the little attorney, who had been in a state of nervous apprehension during the whole interview; "Mr. Pickwick, I beg!"

"I will not be put down, sir," replied Mr. Pickwick hastily.

"Mr. Dodson, you have addressed some remarks to me."

Dodson turned round, bent his head meekly, and smiled.

"Some remarks to me," repeated Mr. Pickwick, almost breathless; "and your partner has tendered me his hand, and you have both assumed a tone of forgiveness and highmindedness, which is an extent of impudence that I was not prepared for, even in you."

"What, sir!" exclaimed Dodson.

"What, sir!" reiterated Fogg.

"Do you know that I have been the victim of your plots and conspiracies?" continued Mr. Pickwick. "Do you know that I am the man whom you have been imprisoning and robbing? Do you know that you were the attorneys for the plaintiff, in *Bardell and Pickwick?*"

"Yes, sir, we do know it," replied Dodson.

"Of course we know it, sir," rejoined Fogg, slapping his pocket—perhaps by accident.

"I see that you recollect it with satisfaction," said Mr. Pickwick, attempting to call up a sneer for the first time in his life, and failing most signally in so doing. "Although I have long been anxious to tell you, in plain terms, what my opinion of you is, I should have let even this opportunity pass, in deference to my friend Perker's wishes, but for the unwarrantable tone you have assumed, and your insolent familiarity. I say insolent familiarity, sir," said Mr. Pickwick, turning upon Fogg with a fierceness of gesture which caused that person to retreat towards the door with great expedition.

"Take care, sir," said Dodson, who, though he was the biggest man of the party, had prudently intrenched himself behind Fogg, and was speaking over his head with a very pale face. "Let him assault you, Mr. Fogg; don't return it on any account."

"No, no, I won't return it," said Fogg, falling back a little more as he spoke; to the evident relief of his partner, who by these means was gradually getting into the outer office.

"You are," continued Mr. Pickwick, resuming the thread of his discourse, "you are a well-matched pair of mean, rascally, pettifogging robbers."

"Well," interposed Perker, "is that all?"

"It is all summed up in that," rejoined Mr. Pickwick; "they are mean, rascally, pettifogging robbers."

"There!" said Perker in a most conciliatory tone. "My dear sirs, he has said all he has to say. Now pray go. Lowten, is that door open?"

Mr. Lowten, with a distant giggle, replied in the affirmative.

"There, there—good morning—good morning—now pray, my dear sirs—Mr. Lowten, the door!" cried the little man, pushing Dodson and Fogg, nothing loath, out of the office; "this way, my dear sirs,—now pray don't prolong this—dear me—Mr. Lowten—the door, sir—why don't you attend?"

"If there's law in England, sir," said Dodson, looking towards Mr. Pickwick, as he put on his hat, "you shall smart for this."

"You are a couple of mean——"

"Remember, sir, you pay dearly for this," said Fogg.

"Rascally, pettifogging robbers!" continued Mr. Pickwick, taking not the least notice of the threats that were addressed to him.

"Robbers!" cried Mr. Pickwick, running to the stair-head, as the two attorneys descended.

"Robbers!" shouted Mr. Pickwick, breaking from Lowten and Perker, and thrusting his head out of the staircase window.

It should be noted that Dodson and Fogg showed a truly Christian spirit, for they took no proceedings for slander against Pickwick, though they might very well have obtained damages.

There is another Christian virtue of Dodson and Fogg, to wit, abstinence, which should not be left unappreciated.

Fogg looked like a man of "vegetable diet" (which Dodson probably thought produced a muddily pallid complexion); but both he and Dodson were far too absorbed in business to drink fermented liquors. After an interview with them Pickwick had to drink a glass of brandy and hot water, and Sam Weller a pint of porter, and even their virtuous client, Mrs. Bardell, and her two female friends drank some exhilarating potion out of a black bottle. Their clerks may out of office hours have joined Mr. Lowten and other solicitors' clerks in spirit-drinking and cigar-smoking; but we are led to infer that Dodson and Fogg never drank anything stronger than water, and that Fogg (if not Dodson) was a vegetarian. Yet there are dreadful hints in Victorian novels that a solicitor like George Meredith's Mr. Thompson would habitually keep a bottle of port in his room and join his clients in drinking it. Indeed, I can remember as long as thirty-five years ago seeing a bottle of brandy on the mantelpiece of a senior partner who kept it available for attacks of "Roman fever" contracted in the course of holiday travels. The melancholy fact, however, remains that (as Mr. Christian writes) "There are none to praise and very few to love" attorneys, and Messrs. Dodson and Fogg illustrate this lack of public appreciation only too well.

I hope that the modern reader is surprised by the eulogy lavished on Dodson and Fogg by respectable solicitors like Perker, for in our day it is more often the layman than the lawyer who admires sharp practice. In all civilisation there has always been a progress in the Law Courts from a blind worship of formulæ to the dictates of equitable common-sense, and even though many reforms are overdue in divorce and police court litigation, some progress has certainly been made in Great Britain during the last hundred years. One must, however, not forget that most men take for granted the virtues of the system in which they are trained, and are even less ready to welcome suggestions of reform with advancing years.

Dodson and Fogg were, of course, created primarily as comic figures, but as often happens with Dickens's creations, their activities raise important issues. Professor Allen has discussed very well in his *Legal Duties* the question how far Law excludes Morality, whether a man may insist on the *jus abutendi*, namely, the exercise of a legal right or how far a lawyer must postpone his client's rights to public policy.

In an ideal society a parliamentary statute might be respected as if it had been carried down on tablets by Moses from Mount Sinai; but although the modern lawyer may have a stronger sense of natural justice than his predecessors, he is certainly more prejudiced against statutes, which appear in more and more chaotic proliferation as time goes on. Moreover, this prejudice is obviously shared by the judges.

Most lawyers, whether ancient or modern, have usually been the watchdogs of liberty and property rights which are more and more restricted by the Fabian and interfering tendencies of modern legislation. It is, therefore, not unnatural that lawyers should feel more loyal to their clients than to the State, and should relish the pleasure of stultifying statutes representing the activities of tyrannical busybodies who ignore and offend public opinion. So long as legislation of this character continues, neither lawyers nor laymen will strongly disapprove the technical skill of attorneys like Dodson and Fogg so long as they do not turn and rend their clients as Dodson and Fogg did with Mrs. Bardell.

Dickens lived in an age when most abuses were anachronisms ripe for destruction like the Fleet prison, whereas the modern law reformer is more concerned with present and future dangers such as the menace of encroaching bureaucracy and the tyranny of irresponsible demagogues.

BOB SAWYER

By J. Johnston Abraham

XII

IT is a commonplace of criticism that every profession considers itself caricatured by the novelist; and it is natural that it should be so, for the imaginative writer, unless he has been educated in some particular calling, is sure to get the minutiæ of that calling wrong.

Now Dickens had an extraordinarily photographic memory for detail—detail of old buildings, queer streets, scenes, faces. His writings abound in accurate descriptions of physical and mental peculiarities. His *street pathology* was often better than that of the doctors of his time. His fat boy, for instance, with his gross body, abnormal appetite, and infinite capacity for sleep is an extremely vivid description of hypo-pituitarism, a condition only recently recognised.

But, though his natural aptitude for observation was admittedly very great, he had not, in 1836, acquired much knowledge of social distinctions; and one is, therefore, not surprised to find that he seems to have had no idea of the great gulf that then existed between the consultant class and the general practitioner—the "poticary," as he was called, somewhat derisively. Indeed even in his later years he still was markedly hazy about such things compared with his contemporary Thackeray. Sir Parker Peps, for example, could never have attained the position Dickens credits him with in *Dombey and Son*. He had none of the qualifications.

The consulting physician of those days was usually a graduate of Oxford or Cambridge, a man of wide learning,

Conviviality at Bob Sawyer's.

and one generally blessed with good family connections—
all of which were necessary to get him inside the close
borough controlling the hospital appointments essential
to his position. Men of the calibre of Sir Henry Halford,
Dr. Pelham Warren, and Sir Thomas Watson represented
the physicians of Pickwick's time. The consulting surgeons
were also drawn from the same class. They were either the
sons or nephews of surgeons already on hospital staffs, or
men who had paid large premiums to be apprenticed to
some hospital surgeon with the ultimate object of attain-
ing a similar position. Abernethy, Sir Everard Home, Sir
Astley Cooper were representative of this class.

Socially below them, in a different category altogether,
were the surgeon-apothecaries or general practitioners.
These men were recruited mainly from the tradesmen or
farmer class. They began their lives as apprentices to an
apothecary, cleaned out the shop, carried the medicines to
the patients' houses, learnt enough Latin to read prescriptions, and were taught by their masters how to compound,
treat coughs and colds, handle minor injuries, bleed,
vaccinate, attend chronic cases, do the after treatment of
midwifery. Thus they learnt gradually all the business of
running a "practice," so that after five to seven years, their
indentures up, they were ready to "walk the hospitals,"
and thus finish their education.

They usually spent a year at hospital, after which they
presented themselves before the Apothecaries Hall, and
sometimes the College of Surgeons in addition, for their
qualifying examination. When they had obtained their
diplomas they generally tried to set up for themselves,
opening a shop where they dispensed drugs over the
counter like a modern chemist, attending the servants and

not infrequently the owners of the great houses, the tradesmen of their neighbourhood, and such of the poor as could
pay them. They never aspired to become physicians or
surgeons, but were quite content to be what they were—
apothecaries, or surgeon-apothecaries, in other words the
general practitioners of the late Georgian and early
Victorian days. Their education was mainly that of the
apprentice, and it was very practical. Indeed, many of
them never tried to learn any more than their apprenticeship taught them, for it is on record that in 1853 out of
33,000 practitioners not more than 11,000 were actually
legally qualified. The other twenty-two thousand were in
the same position as most dentists some thirty years ago—
good practical men without any academic training.

Almost all the doctors in Dickens's novels belonged to
this general practitioner class; and the medical students in
Pickwick were all training for it. A considerable number of
medical men appear and reappear in the novels; but not
one of them is more than a minor character. There are no
doctor villains, lovers, or heroes in any of his romances.
He does not go out of his way to castigate the profession
as he does the lawyers, or hold it up to ridicule like the
sectarians of the Little Bethels. On the whole, doctors
come off well. He does not flatter them. He does not abuse
them. They are just pleasantly and whimsically caricatured
with the little touch of exaggeration that is typically
Dickensian. Dr. Bayham Badger, "Mrs. Bayham Badger's
third," is a fair average practitioner, a bit of a sycophant.
Mr. Jobling is definitely a rogue. Mr. Chillip, the gentle
little man who helped David Copperfield into the world,
is the typical village practitioner beloved of rich and poor
alike. Fat Mr. Losberne, who "set" Oliver Twist's arm, is

pleasantly competent. They all stand out clearly. They are nothing much to boast about, just average men with their outlook a little elevated above the tradesman class by the fact that they are making their living out of alleviating pain and suffering, not selling groceries.

Most of them kept shops where anyone could buy a pennyworth of castor oil or a box of pills over the counter. Such men were the general practitioners of Pickwick's day, before the passing of the Medical Act of 1858 which abolished the Olympian exclusiveness of the consultant class, killed the monopoly of the Royal Colleges, and compelled every doctor to go through the same curriculum and pass a standardised examination—in other words, become a general practitioner first—before he could aspire to the higher position of consultant. It seems odd to us now that it should ever have been otherwise. But the same distinction still exists in the law between barristers and solicitors; and because we are used to this we accept it as natural.

Dickens, when he wrote *The Pickwick Papers,* had no actual knowledge of the consultant class. But he did know the medical students and the hag-nurses of his time. That is why his Bob Sawyer and Benjamin Allen, his Sairey Gamp and Betsy Prig still conjure up pictures that have passed into the category of living personalities. They are more alive, owing to the alchemy of his imagination, than many who have actually trodden the earth.

It was at Dingley Dell on Christmas morning that Mr. Pickwick first made the acquaintance of Mr. Bob Sawyer.

Sam Weller had brought the hot water to Mr. Pickwick's bedroom.

"Sir. There's a couple o' Sawbones downstairs," he said, by way of morning gossip.

"A couple of what?" exclaimed Mr. Pickwick, sitting up in bed.

"A couple o' Sawbones," said Sam.

"What's a Sawbones?" inquired the innocent Mr. Pickwick.

"I thought everybody know'd as a Sawbones was a surgeon," replied Sam; adding that "These here ones as is below, though, ain't reg'ler thorough-bred Sawbones; they're only in trainin'," in other words "medical students."

Mr. Pickwick with his usual benevolence seems to have thought highly of the medical profession, and even of the medical student.

"I am glad of it," said Mr. Pickwick, casting his night-cap energetically on the counterpane. "They are fine fellows; very fine fellows; with judgments matured by observation and reflection; tastes refined by reading and study. I am very glad of it."

But Sam, with perhaps a closer and more cynical know-ledge of the world, was not so sure of these advantages.

"They're a smokin' cigars by the kitchen fire," he said.

"Ah!" observed Mr. Pickwick, rubbing his hands, "overflowing with kindly feelings and animal spirits. Just what I like to see."

"And one on 'em," said Sam, not noticing his master's interruption, "one on 'em's got his legs on the table, and is a drinkin' brandy neat; vile the t'other one—him in the barnacles [spectacles]—has got a barrel o' oysters atween his knees, wich he's a openin' like steam, and as fast as he eats 'em, he takes a aim vith the shells at young dropsy [the fat boy] who's a sittin' down fast asleep in the chimbley corner."

"Eccentricities of genius, Sam," said Mr. Pickwick. "You may retire."

And so Mr. Bob Sawyer comes on the scene, with his spectacled friend Mr. Benjamin Allen, the brother of Arabella, "the young lady with fur round her boots" whom Bob is supposed to be courting, but who has already given her heart to Mr. Winkle. Both of them were training to be general practitioners.

Now in Mr. Pickwick's time the general practitioner, as may be appreciated from what has gone before, was a man of little learning and less culture, for he was apprenticed at the age of fifteen, and unless he had a good master, his education, apart from the practical details of his calling, then ceased. The young men who "walked the hospitals" at the conclusion of their apprenticeship were not always, therefore, models to be admired, according to contemporary fiction. Albert Smith, for instance, who was himself in the profession, had not a good word to say for them; and Thackeray in *Pendennis* makes Huxter an uninviting character. But it is through the portraits painted by Dickens of Bob and his friends that they are now generally remembered.

Medical writers have complained that these young men appear to have been drawn rather from the raffish heroes of Pierce Egan, Jerry and Tom, than from life, and that they represent not so much medicine as the idle apprentices of any of the black-coated callings. They take umbrage at the fact that Bob Sawyer and Benjamin Allen are represented as untidy in their habits, with dubious linen, and in a constant state of inebriety. It must be remembered, however, that on the morning of their first appearance they were recovering from a "night out" at the Blue Lion at

Muggleton, "where the brandy was too good to leave in a hurry." Moreover, descriptions of alcoholic excess were considered very funny even up to the end of the Victorian period, and no one thought any the worse of his friends for getting drunk occasionally. Dickens, who was a man of his time, reflects this feeling when he allows his hero, Mr. Pickwick, to get so fuddled on cold punch that he was unconscious when Captain Bolding ordered him to be wheeled to the village pound and dumped there. No doubt, then, the medical students that he knew not infrequently overstepped the mark. And why not! It would be hypocritical to maintain that medical students did not conform to type, for it has always been a sign of youth and inexperience to boast of the amount of alcohol a man could hold; and, if my memory serves me aright, it was not an unknown habit amongst medical and other students even in Edwardian days.

Certainly in some respects human nature has not changed much since Dickens's time, for even now the callow "first year" man has the same desire to make the flesh of the layman creep. Dickens obviously knew the symptom.

"Nothing like dissecting to give one an appetite," said Mr. Bob Sawyer looking round the table.

Mr. Pickwick slightly shuddered.

"By the by, Bob," said Mr. Allen, "have you finished that leg yet?"

"Nearly," replied Sawyer, helping himself to half a fowl as he spoke. "It's a very muscular one for a child's."

"Is it?" said Mr. Allen carelessly.

"Very," said Bob, with his mouth full.

"I've put myself down for an arm at my place," said Mr. Allen.

"We're clubbing for a subject, and the list is nearly full, only we can't get hold of any fellow that wants a head. I wish you'd take it."

"No," replied Bob Sawyer; "can't afford expensive luxuries."

"Nonsense!" said Allen.

"Can't indeed," rejoined Bob Sawyer. "I wouldn't mind a brain, but I couldn't stand a whole head."

"Hush, hush, gentlemen, pray," said Mr. Pickwick, "I hear the ladies."

It was little wonder the chivalrous Mr. Pickwick did not care to have the question of anatomy discussed before the ladies, for dissecting rooms and the need for dissection was a very burning question in 1836, and the exploits of the Resurrection Men, and the horrors of the Burke and Hare murders were still fresh in the public mind. It is a long forgotten story now; but it was not so in those days.

For centuries dissection could be carried on in this country legally only on the bodies of condemned criminals. This was always a great handicap to knowledge, but it did not become really acute until towards the end of the eighteenth century, when medical education was advancing rapidly and students required a more expert knowledge of anatomy than formerly. At that time, too, owing to the constant wars of the Napoleonic period, and the rapid expansion of our colonies, there was a great demand for surgeons in the army and navy, and all the medical schools were more than full of students.

Consequently, the procuring of bodies, or "subjects" as they were called, became a matter of extreme importance to the schools if they wished to attract and retain students.

Bodies of unclaimed paupers thus came to be worth five to ten pounds; and there were not wanting workhouse officials, sextons, undertakers, and graveyard keepers quite willing to dispose of such "subjects" to the medical schools, particularly as no questions were asked.

City graveyards in those days were full to overflowing; and bodies were often buried very lightly so as not to disturb the coffins and bones underneath. It was an easy mental step for the gravediggers just to cover a body at the funeral, disinter it rapidly the same night, and hand it over to some intermediary between them and the medical schools before dawn.

It was thus that the Resurrection Men, or body-snatchers, arose. As a class they were a British institution, for on the Continent material for dissection was amply provided for by law. They were usually men of the lowest type, human ghouls who squandered their ill-gotten gains in drink. They worked in gangs and rival gangs, fighting one another for the bodies of the dead, even in the very graveyards, and blackmailing the teachers of anatomy with impunity, for there were never enough "subjects" to supply the demand.

Eleven hundred and fifty criminals were executed in Great Britain between 1805 and 1820. That is about seventy-six a year, all the legal material available. But there were more than a thousand students in London alone, and nearly as many in Edinburgh and Dublin, all of them wanting dissecting parts. Little wonder the "Resurrectionists" had it all their own way with the doctors. It was an intolerable situation, and things were more than ripe for a change. But it was not until the murders committed by Burke and Hare in Edinburgh in 1828, and by Bishop,

Williams, and May in London in 1831, finally roused the
public that anything could be done. Burke and the others
named could not even wait for people to die. They mur-
dered in order to obtain "subjects" for sale to the medical
schools; and it was the outcry over these atrocities that
compelled Parliament reluctantly to intervene. As a consequence the Anatomy Act of 1832 was passed, and the
horrible occupation of the body-snatchers thus ended.
That is why when the Pickwick Papers were appearing in
1836 Mr. Bob Sawyer had an interested audience whenever
he mentioned the dissecting room.

There is no doubt Dickens knew his medical students
much better than many of his critics will admit, for he
sketches in very neatly some of their salient characteristics.
There is Mr. Benjamin Allen's anxiety to bleed the unfortunate Winkle when he fell on the ice; there is the same
boasting of the skill of one's hospital chief and the marvel-
lous operations at which one has helped; and there is the
same unmerciful "pulling the leg" of the uninitiated that
exists even unto this day. Mr. Bob Sawyer and Mr.
Benjamin Allen were Guy's men; and Bob gave his
famous supper to Mr. Pickwick at his rooms in the
Borough. To this party came Mr. Jack Hopkins of St.
Bartholomew's.

"You're late, Jack," said Mr. Benjamin Allen.

"Been detained at Bartholomew's," replied Hopkins.

"Anything new?"

"No, nothing particular. Rather a good accident
brought into the Casualty Ward."

"What was that, sir?" inquired Mr. Pickwick.

"Only a man fallen out of a four pair of stairs window;
—but it's a very fair case—very fair case indeed."

"Do you mean that the patient is in a fair way to recover?" inquired Mr. Pickwick.

"No," replied Hopkins carelessly. "No. I should rather say he wouldn't. There must be a splendid operation though to-morrow—magnificent sight if Slasher does it."

"You consider Mr. Slasher a good operator?" said Mr. Pickwick.

"Best alive," replied Hopkins. "Took a boy's leg out of the socket last week—boy ate five apples and a gingerbread cake—exactly two minutes after it was all over, boy said he wouldn't lie there to be made game of, and he'd tell his mother if they didn't begin."

"Dear me!" said Mr. Pickwick, astonished.

"Pooh! That's nothing, that ain't," said Jack Hopkins. "Is it, Bob?"

"Nothing at all," replied Mr. Bob Sawyer.

"By the way, Bob," said Hopkins, with a scarcely perceptible glance at Mr. Pickwick's attentive face, "we had a curious accident last night. A child was brought in who had swallowed a necklace."

"Swallowed what, sir?" interrupted Mr. Pickwick.

And then follows the diverting story of how the child swallowed one bead after another until he had finished the whole necklace, and began to rattle inside. "He's in the hospital now," said Jack Hopkins, "and he makes such a devil of a noise when he walks about, that they're obliged to muffle him in a watchman's coat for fear he should wake the patients."

"That's the most extraordinary case I ever heard of," said Mr. Pickwick, with an emphatic blow on the table.

"Oh, that's nothing," said Jack Hopkins. "Is it, Bob?"

"Certainly not," replied Mr. Bob Sawyer.

"Very singular things occur in our profession, I can assure you, sir," said Hopkins.

"So I should be disposed to imagine," replied Mr. Pickwick.

There you have an accurate caricature, drawn with all the inimitable skill of the master, of just how the student's mind looks upon an accident, just how he venerates his chief, and just how he tries to gull with tall stories anyone sufficiently simple to believe him.

Mr. Bob Sawyer was in very low financial water when he gave his party and very much at the mercy of his landlady, Mrs. Raddle. When we meet him next he was still in financial difficulties. But in the interval he has managed to pass the "Hall" and "College" and become a full-blown surgeon-apothecary, practising at Bristol. It was there accordingly that, some months later, his unsuspected rival in the affections of Miss Arabella found him, with a shop and a surgery of his own labelled: "Sawyer, late Nockemorf."

Bob was now a "studious looking young gentleman in green spectacles"; and Mr. Winkle may be forgiven for not recognising him until he threw off his disguise, hauled him into the surgery behind the shop, reintroduced him to Mr. Benjamin Allen, and made him partake of some of the firm's "patent digester"—a black bottle half full of brandy.

"What a very nice place you have here," said Mr. Winkle.

"Pretty well. Pretty well," replied Bob Sawyer. "I 'passed' soon after that precious party, and my friends came down with the needful for the business; so I put on a black suit of clothes, and a pair of spectacles, and came here to look as solemn as I could."

But things had not been going too well with Mr. Sawyer. He got lots of patients, but unfortunately they forgot to pay him. His stock of drugs was very meagre, and most of the drawers in his shop, with their labels and little gilt knobs, were only dummies. None the less he was as cheerful and full of boisterous fun as ever. When his apprentice came in to tell him that he had delivered all the medicines, Winkle, who had been listening to his tale of woe, remarked:

"Come, things are not quite so bad as you would have me believe, either. There is some medicine to be sent out."

Mr. Bob Sawyer peeped into the shop to see that no stranger was within hearing, and leaning forward to Mr. Winkle said, in a low tone:

"He leaves it all at the wrong houses."

Mr. Winkle looked perplexed, and Bob and his friend laughed.

"Don't you see?" said Bob. "He goes to a house, rings the area bell, pokes a packet of medicine without a direction into the servant's hand, and walks off. Servant takes it into the dining parlour, master opens it and reads the label:

"Draught to be taken at bedtime—pills as before—lotion as usual—the powder. From Sawyer's late Nockemorf's. Physicians' prescriptions carefully prepared," and all the rest of it. Shows it to his wife—she reads the label; it goes down to the servants—they read the label. Next day boy calls: very sorry—his mistake—immense business—great many parcels to deliver—Mr. Sawyer's compliments—late Nockemorf." The name gets known, and that's the thing, my boy, in the medical way. Bless your heart, old fellow, it's better than all the advertising in the world. We have got one four-ounce bottle that's been to half the houses in Bristol, and hasn't done yet."

"Dear me, I see," observed Mr. Winkle. "What an excellent plan."

"Oh, Ben and I have hit upon a dozen such," replied Bob Sawyer with great glee. "The lamplighter has eighteenpence a week to pull the night bell for ten minutes every time he comes round; and my boy always rushes into church just before the psalms, when the people have nothing to do but look round 'em, and calls me out with horror and dismay depicted on his countenance. 'Bless my soul,' everybody says, 'somebody's taken suddenly ill! Sawyer late Nockemorf sent for. What a business that young man has!'"

At the termination of this disclosure of some of the mysteries of medicine, Mr. Bob Sawyer and his friend Ben Allen threw themselves back in their respective chairs, and laughed boisterously.

It is clear from all this that Mr. Bob had been studying his Smollett and the methods of Count Fathom even more carefully than his Celsus. Or perhaps it was Dickens!

In spite of all this ingenuity, however, the practice did not prosper, at any rate financially.

"It's wonderful how the poor people patronise me," said Mr. Bob Sawyer reflectively. "They knock me up at all hours of the night; they take medicine to an extent which I should have conceived impossible; they put on blisters and leeches with a perseverance worthy of a better cause; they make additions to their families in a manner which is quite awful. Six of those last-named little promissory notes, all due on the same day, Ben, and all entrusted to me."

"It's very gratifying, isn't it?" said Mr. Ben Allen, holding his plate for some more minced veal.

"Oh, very," replied Bob. "Only not quite so much so as the confidence of patients with a shilling or two to spare would be. This business was capitally described in the advertisement, Ben. It's a practice, a very extensive practice—and that's all."

Obviously things were in a bad way and required desperate remedies. It was Mr. Ben Allen who suggested the solution: immediate marriage between his sister, Arabella, and Mr. Sawyer, not knowing the young lady had already eloped with our Mr. Winkle.

But Bob had no illusions on the subject.

"She's a very charming and very delightful creature," quoth Mr. Bob Sawyer, "and has only one fault that I know of, Ben. It happens, unfortunately, that that single blemish is a want of taste. She don't like me."

And so he was not heartbroken when Miss Arabella's aunt arrived at the surgery, followed closely by Mr. Pickwick and the inevitable Sam Weller, each intent on breaking the news of the marriage of Miss Allen and Mr. Winkle to the parties concerned. Indeed, after Mr. Pickwick's soothing explanations aided by close application "several times to the mouth of a black bottle, Bob's features gradually assumed a cheerful and even jovial expression. And at last he emerged from the room, bottle in hand, and remarking that he was very sorry to say he had been making a fool of himself, begged to propose the health and happiness of Mr. and Mrs. Winkle, whose felicity so far from envying, he would be the first to congratulate them upon."

And that was that. Evidently Bob was not of the type

that hankered after woman's company. Indeed, we cannot imagine him as anything but a bachelor.

But the last hope of rescuing the practice was now gone; and so, with his usual impetuosity and whimsical outlook, he decided to clear out of Bristol forthwith.

That was why Mr. Pickwick found Bob's apprentice putting up the shutters of "Sawyer late Nockemorf," when he called on his way to Birmingham next morning in his post chaise to pick up Mr. Ben Allen.

"What's the matter?" said Mr. Pickwick to the boy.

"Nothing's the matter, sir," replied the boy.

"All right, all right!" cried Bob Sawyer, suddenly appearing in the door. "I'm going, old fellow."

"You?" exclaimed Mr. Pickwick.

"Yes," replied Bob Sawyer, "and a regular expedition we'll make of it. Here, Sam! Look out!" Thus briefly bespeaking Mr. Weller's attention, Mr. Bob Sawyer jerked his leathern knapsack into the dickey, where it was immediately stowed away under the seat by Sam, who regarded the proceedings with great admiration.

"My dear sir," said Mr. Pickwick, with some embarrassment, "I had no idea of your accompanying us."

"No, that's just the very thing," replied Bob, seizing Mr. Pickwick by the lapel of his coat. "That's the joke."

"Bless me, you're surely not mad enough to think of leaving your patients without anybody to attend them?" remonstrated Mr. Pickwick in a serious tone.

"Why not?" answered Bob. "I shall save by it, you know. None of them ever pay. Besides," he said, lowering his voice to a confidential whisper, "they will be all the better for it; for being nearly out of drugs, and not able to increase my account just now, I should have been obliged to give them calomel all round, and it would have been certain to have disagreed with some of them. So, it's all for the best."

"But this chaise, my young friend, will only hold two; and I am pledged to Mr. Allen," said the embarrassed Mr. Pickwick.

"Don't think of me for a minute," replied Bob. "I've arranged it all. Sam and I will share the dickey between us. Look here. This little bill is to be wafered on the shop door. ' Sawyer, late Nockemorf, inquire of Mrs. Cripps over the way.' Mrs. Cripps is my boy's mother. 'Mr. Sawyer's very sorry,' says Mrs. Cripps, 'couldn't help it—fetched away early this morning to a consultation of the very first surgeons in the country—couldn't do without him—would have him at any price—tremendous operation.' The fact is," said Bob in conclusion, "it'll do me more good than otherwise, I expect. If it gets into one of the local papers it will be the making of me. Here's Ben; now then, jump in."

Bob thereupon mounted to the dickey beside Sam Weller, and the chaise proceeded on its way to Birmingham. Whilst they were in the city Bob kept quiet and sedate; but when they emerged on the open road he "threw off his green spectacles and his gravity together" and started making merry, waving a crimson silk pocket handkerchief tied to a stick, and imitating a key-bugle to the great joy of all the passers-by.

"I wonder," said Mr. Pickwick, stopping in the middle of a most sedate conversation with Mr. Allen, "I wonder what all the people we pass can see in us to make them stare so?"

Mr. Allen suggested that it might be due to the elegance of the equipage. But Mr. Pickwick had his doubts.

"I hope," he said, "that our volatile friend is committing no absurdities in that dickey behind."

"Oh dear no," replied Ben Allen. "Except when he's elevated, Bob's the quietest creature breathing."

Mr. Pickwick still had his doubts; and when he once more heard a prolonged imitation of a key-bugle he put his head out of the chaise window. What he saw was "Mr. Bob Sawyer seated not in the dickey but on the roof of the chaise, with his legs as far asunder as they would conveniently go, wearing Mr. Samuel Weller's hat on one side of his head, and bearing in one hand a most enormous sandwich, while in the other he supported a goodly-sized case bottle to both of which he applied himself with intense relish: varying the monotony of the occupation by an occasional howl or the interchange of some lively badinage with any passing stranger. The crimson flag was carefully tied in an erect position to the rail of the dickey; and Mr. Samuel Weller, decorated with Bob's hat, was seated in the centre thereof, discussing a twin sandwich with an animated countenance the expression of which betokened his entire and perfect approval of the whole arrangement."

"Mr. Sawyer!" cried Mr. Pickwick in a state of great excitement. "Mr. Sawyer, sir!"

"Hallo!" responded that gentleman, looking over the side of the chaise with all the coolness in life.

"Are you mad, sir?" demanded Mr. Pickwick.

"Not a bit of it," replied Bob, "only cheerful."

"Cheerful, sir!" ejaculated Mr. Pickwick. "Take down that scandalous red handkerchief, I beg, I insist, sir. Sam, take it down!"

Bob complied, took a long drink at the case bottle, and nodded smiling at Mr. Pickwick.

"Come," said Mr. Pickwick, whose momentary anger was not quite proof against Bob's immovable self-possession, "pray let us have no more of this absurdity."

"Oh certainly," said Bob, "it's not the sort of thing at all. All over, governor."

That satisfied Mr. Pickwick, and he withdrew his head inside the chaise. But presently he noticed something on a string tapping at the window.

"What's this?" exclaimed Mr. Pickwick.

"It looks like a case-bottle," exclaimed Mr. Allen.

"What's to be done?" said Mr. Pickwick.

"I think it would be best to take it in," said Mr. Allen. "It would serve him right to take it in and keep it."

"It would," said Mr. Pickwick. "Shall I?"

"I think it the most proper course we could possibly adopt," said Mr. Allen; and this coinciding with Mr. Pickwick's opinion he "gently let down the window and disengaged the bottle from the stick, upon which the latter was drawn up, and Mr. Bob Sawyer was heard to laugh heartily."

"What a merry dog it is," said Mr. Pickwick looking round at his companion with the bottle in his hand.

"He is," said Mr. Allen.

"You cannot possibly be angry with him," said Mr. Pickwick.

"Quite out of the question," observed Mr. Allen.

The bottle they discovered after some discreet research contained milk-punch, one of Mr. Pickwick's little weaknesses.

"It would serve him right," said Mr. Pickwick with some severity, "it would serve him right to drink it, every drop."

"The very thing that occurred to me," said Ben Allen.

"Is it indeed?" rejoined Mr. Pickwick. "Then, here's his health." He took an energetic pull at the bottle, Mr. Allen followed him; and smiling mutually the milk punch was finally disposed of.

"After all," said Mr. Pickwick, as he drained the last drop, "his pranks are really very amusing, very entertaining indeed."

"You may say that," rejoined Mr. Ben Allen.

All the same he was not quite the companion Mr. Pickwick would have chosen, had he had his way, to support him at his interview with Mr. Winkle, senior—the object of his journey to Birmingham. And Mr. Sawyer's behaviour at the interview certainly did not help that rather prim gentleman to view his son's unexpected marriage with Arabella more favourably.

None the less they came through it, surviving also the wet discomforts of the return journey to London, enlivened as it was by the fierce battle between Mr. Pott of the Eatanswill Gazette, and Mr. Slurk of the Eatanswill Independent at the Saracen's Head at Towcester. Mr. Pickwick tried, of course, to keep the peace between the combatants there with considerable risk to himself. But the two young apothecaries merely took a scientific interest in the fray, "dodging round the group, each with a tortoise-shell lancet in his hand, ready to bleed the first man stunned."

After this we lose sight of Mr. Bob Sawyer, except as a name at the marriage of Mr. Snodgrass, for Dickens by now was drawing the threads of his narrative together for the final pairing-off scenes between the lovers, and Bob was decidedly not one of these. We may perhaps be allowed to think that he would have made a more virile husband for Arabella than the wishy-washy Mr. Winkle. But Dickens evidently felt he was not built for matrimony.

We feel, none the less, that he had got to like him better as he came to know him better. It is a way novelists have, and we can sympathise with the weakness. We are therefore relieved to learn that Bob and his *fidus Achates* eventually solved their difficulties by obtaining medical appointments from the East India Company in Bengal; and we are glad to find that they flourished there. It is true Dickens makes them each get yellow fever fourteen times, thus curing them of their love for alcohol; and it does not matter that yellow fever does not occur in India and a second attack of it is practically unknown. Dickens was just muddling India with the West Indies and malaria with yellow fever. But that is the way of novelists.

Bob and his sort have vanished from the hospitals. The Medical Act of 1858, by compelling all would-be consultants first to qualify as medical practitioners, raised the status of the medical student to what it is to-day. The old-time apothecary with his shop and glass counter, his gallipots, galenicals, and his apprentices is no more. In some ways this is to be regretted, for he was a practical man who knew all about the drugs he dispensed for his patients—much more so than the modern doctor; and his apprentices were taught how to earn their living, a thing the modern doctor has had to learn painfully after qualification. But time and progress were against him; and he is now an almost forgotten memory. Bob Sawyer thus represents a phase of late Georgian and early Victorian life that is no more. To-day his type is as extinct as the Sairey Gamps who have been superseded by the trim young disciples of Florence Nightingale. Yet such is the intense feeling of reality produced by the genius of Dickens that he comes to life afresh—bibulous, boisterous, good-natured—every time we take up again the immortal adventures of Mr. Pickwick.

THE FAT BOY

By Arthur Waugh

XIII

"THE Influence of Obesity upon Character" might well have been the theme of one of the Posthumous Papers of the Pickwick Club, for the question came up for debate before ever the features of the immortal Samuel Pickwick himself first beamed a benediction on the world. The occasion is familiar to all good Dickensians. Robert Seymour, the ill-starred artist, who was to die by his own hand a few weeks later, had submitted a trial sketch or two of the Pickwick of his own imagination. They showed the figure of a tall, thin man, eagerly, pertinaciously alert. "No, no," exclaimed Edward Chapman, a publisher who, unlike most of his tribe, knew what he wanted. "This Pickwick is to be a hearty man, a jovial fellow, companionable, jocund. Pickwick must be fat, quite definitely fat. Flesh and good humour have gone together always since the days of Falstaff." His hearers ruminated, and agreed. They reminded themselves, perhaps, of Sir Toby Belch, of Sancho Panza, of Friar Tuck, and of many another "plump and pleasing person." Obesity and good fellowship were indeed inseparable. So Seymour's Slender was scrapped; a genial buck from Richmond was exhibited as a model; and Mr. Pickwick emerged with his comfortable paunch, his drab tights, and black gaiters, surmounted by the flashing spectacles and friendly smile of the most popular character in all the range of English fiction.

And what of the author's opinion? "There lives no record of reply." Presumably Charles Dickens, like the

Mary and the fat boy.

mother of Chevalier's Little Nipper, "wasn't raising no objection," for the Pickwick of the author's invention was at once the Pickwick of his publisher's programme. All the same, there rankled in the background of his memory the vision of another fat figure, who was not so amiable, so simple-minded, and so alert. And by way, as it were, of counterblast, he set over against the good nature of chubby Mr. Pickwick the drowsy, menacing obesity of the Fat Boy, who may have made his own boyish pilgrimages uncomfortable, as he went to and fro upon his lawful occasions in the mean thoroughfares of Chatham.

For Mr. Wardle's Joe was drawn from life. His name was James Budden, and his father kept the Red Lion Inn at the corner of High Street and Military Road, in the Chatham days of John Dickens's anxious conflict with the "myrmidons of the law." The Red Lion had a notable rival in the Mitre Inn and Clarence Hotel, which in 1838 was used to boast itself "the first posting-house in the town." The fat James Budden may well have been jealous of the honour of his father's house, no less than of the popularity of a certain small boy, Charles Dickens, whose father was a constant patron of the other establishment. For Mr. Tribe, the proprietor of the Mitre, thought no small things of young Charles's singing, and found that his skill could be employed as a bait to his own bar-parlour. So he set the boy Dickens on the table, and made him sing old sea-songs to amuse the tippling sailors on the benches round. The entertainment proved a "draw"; and no doubt John Dickens, the father, who was never too proud to accept a helping hand, got as many free drinks as he could carry, out of compliment to his son. If James Budden, waiting at the corner of Military Road, to catch the little

Charles on his way to school, took toll of him for his minstrelsy, the novelist-that-was-to-be had not forgotten the grudge. "Pickwick" had not advanced far in its progress before James Budden made his appearance in its pages; and, as we shall shortly have cause to discover, he would hardly have relished a portrait which he could scarcely have failed to recognise.

2

Nobody will have forgotten the Fat Boy's first appearance. Like so many doubtful blessings, he displayed at first the features of a heaven-sent benefactor.

It was the day of the military review at Rochester, when all the townsfolk rose early from their beds, to see half a dozen regiments, "with their usual shallo-humps and shallo-hoops," engaging in a sham fight of astonishing vigour under "the eagle eye of the commander-in-chief." It was always Mr. Pickwick's way to be in the forefront of an affair like this; and so persistent was his curiosity that he and his companions soon found themselves in the direct path of the advancing troops, and forced to beat a most undignified retreat, right across the field of battle. Off blew Mr. Pickwick's hat; off rushed Mr. Pickwick in its pursuit, until it finally landed under the wheels of the commodious barouche, where Mr. Wardle, a stout old gentleman in a blue coat, corduroy breeches, and top-boots was entertaining a cheerful company of evenly-assorted sex to one of those liberal feasts which the Pickwickians were never reluctant to share. The stout gentleman was Mr. Wardle (another instance of obese good-nature), and on the box of the vehicle sat a still stouter boy, fast asleep, his hands in his pockets, his red face sunk upon his breast.

"Joe! Damn that boy—he's gone to sleep again," cried Mr. Wardle. "Joe, let down the steps!"

Joe woke as readily as he slumbered, and was soon busy, handing round the knives, forks, and plates—only to fall asleep again, until the word "eatables" awoke a horrible leer in his eyes; and the tongue, the pigeon-pie, the veal and ham, the lobsters and the salad, sent him off again, to dream of Lucullan banquets, in which it was his lot to have first choice of the tit-bits, instead of foraging among the broken fragments.

He was greedy? Of course he was greedy; but who can blame him for that? For what he was about to receive, he was always truly thankful; and even the teetotal dietetic professes that modest grace, with much less cause for gratitude. Besides he was merely obeying the call of nature, as the poet and the "hiker" habitually do. So vast a form as his needed more than mortal sustenance to keep it equal to its task. And, having fed, he displayed a rigid restraint. He never made a beast of himself. He simply slept again, as every fat man has, when his meal was over, since the days of Ehud and Eglon. He never forgot his place. He never talked. He took no liberties, and cut no capers. No sooner was he at leisure than an innocent and impenetrable somnolence absorbed him; *O si sic omnes!* . . .

> Of all the ills beneath the sun,
> Say, which in morning sleep was done?

3

But it must not be imagined that Joe's tastes were exclusively sumptuary. If they had been, he would not have kept his place for a month under Mr. Wardle's "hospitable roof" at Manor Farm, Dingley Dell. Mr. Wardle would appear to have had a sort of obsession of hospitality. Everybody he met was at once invited to stay with him for the longest week-end in the calendar. Mr. Pickwick's hat having blown under Mr. Wardle's wheels, it followed, "as the night the day," that Mr. Pickwick and all his company must "blow in" to Mr. Wardle's corridor-full of spare rooms, and taste the riches of his apparently inexhaustible larder. Food and drink to-night; and with to-morrow's dawn, sport. There were rooks in the spinney, and the time for shooting them had come. At the first whisper of a "battue," the Fat Boy's eyes glistened, and he was as much awake as he could ever be—which is to say that "he did not appear more than three parts and a fraction asleep."

Make no mistake about it, the Fat Boy was at heart a sportsman.

It is the first distinction of the true sportsman that he wants all the world to share his enjoyment. Does the fox-hunter sneak off alone to the covert? No, he is never happy without a full field, and a crowded breakfast table. "We'll all go a hunting to-day," he cries, and brandishes his hunting crop at the casements of the lie-abeds. In precisely the same spirit the inimitable Joe set to work on the morning of the rook-shooting. He determined that no one should miss the fun. Mr. Winkle, heavily burdened with his un-merited reputation as a sportsman, was the only Pick-

wickian whom the Fat Boy had been ordered to call at the
very early hour when the shooting was to begin. But in
his exuberant excitement he called everybody indis-
criminately. And so, like the innumerable company of
sportsmen whose keenness leads them into excesses—the
leg theory bowlers and all the rest of the crew—he laid up
for himself disaster and distress. If only he had not called
Mr. Tupman, what trouble might have been averted! He
had not been ordered to call Mr. Tupman. Mr. Tupman,
no doubt, did not want to be called. He had revelled over-
night, and would fain have dreamed out his romantic
dreams to an end. But the Fat Boy called him, and Fate set
him in Mr. Winkle's line of fire. While the Fat Boy was
picking up the game, with a glitter in his sporting eye,
which only a cynic could attribute to a vision of rook-pie,
Mr. Tupman was relinquishing his wounded arm to the
care of the sympathetic ladies of Manor Farm, and returning with interest the romantic gaze of Miss Rachael, most
sympathetic and tenderest of them all. It may well be that
the Fat Boy was himself a romanticist, with a fleeting gift
of prophecy. For romance was blossoming in Manor
Farm; and it was the Fat Boy's fate to be its swift and
mischievous harbinger.

4

It was Mr. Wardle's way to provide entertainment for
his guests from day to day; and after the rook-shooting
came the great cricket match between All-Muggleton and
Dingley Dell. All the men of the party decided to walk
over—all, that is to say, except Mr. Tupman, whose

wounded arm was left to the care of the ladies at home. And one boy, a fat one, remained at home as well. Perhaps it was the length of the walk; for, though it lay through shady lanes and sequestered footpaths, two miles is two miles, and a spreading waist-line is a sad handicap to exercise. When the Fat Boy travelled, he travelled behind horses.

So Joe missed the fervours of the famous match; the insidious attack of Mr. Luffey; the stolid defence of Mr. Dumkins; and above all the "devilish good dinner—cold but capital," to which the slim and volatile Mr. Jingle did more than justice, both in words and deeds. Alas for the disabilities of obesity! Poor Joe was asleep at home, dreaming, no doubt, after a surfeit of pie, "cold but capital," of "the many-wintered crow that leads the clanging rookery home."

There was another side to his character, however, which was not to be denied. The Fat Boy was a moral romanticist; and, while the rest of the company was revelling round the green sward, there was a romance brewing in the quiet seclusion of Dingley Dell, of which Joe himself was to be the first, inquisitive, rather nasty-minded observer. For Mr. Tupman, having added the appeal of a suffering hero to his familiar prowess as a lady-killer, was once more engaged in one of his wicked little games, with Miss Rachael Wardle, sister of his absent host, as willing victim. Willing indeed she was; for it was she who led the way to a bower of honey-suckle and jessamine, where "chorussed nature" whispered of love, and Mr. Tupman translated its mystic poetry into fervid, unmistakable prose.

"Miss Wardle," he said, "you are an angel."

What woman of mature years could resist so original a sentiment?

"Mr. Tupman," she faltered, "I can hardly speak the words—but—but—you are not wholly indifferent to me."

Was this boldness? Was it unmaidenly? Mr. Tupman did not pause to question. He seized the lady in his arms; and, after an interval of seemly struggle and resistance, closed her lips with a cataract of kisses. "Now was she in the very lists of love." The situation was perilous. But the prying avenger of the proprieties was at hand. A shadow fell across the entrance of the bower.

"There was the fat boy, perfectly motionless, with his large circular eyes staring into the arbour, but without the slightest expression on his face that the most expert physiognomist could have referred to astonishment, curiosity, or any other known passion that agitates the human breast."

"Supper's ready, sir," said Joe, with the imperturbable detachment of the perfectly-trained domestic servant. And then he stood aside, to let the fluttering lovers pass from poetry to prose, from the couch of love to the table of refreshment.

"He knows nothing of what has happened," whispered Mr. Tupman.

"Nothing," echoed his fair lady, with eyes downcast.

What was that sudden sound behind them? Surely not a chuckle? "No; it could not have been the Fat Boy; there was not a gleam of mirth, nor anything but feeding, in his whole visage."

"He must have been fast asleep," said Mr. Tupman; and the guilty couple laughed with answering eyes. But they were laughing too soon. For once the Fat Boy had been wide awake.

It was a silent supper; for the merry revellers had not yet returned. And it was a long evening before their voices were heard in the drive; and surely there was something strange in their tones. A stranger's voice among them also.

"Nothing the matter, ma'am," replied the stranger. "Cricket dinner—glorious party—capital songs—old port, claret, good, very good." Mr. Jingle had attached himself to the party. Mr. Jingle was drunk. Everybody was drunk. Mr. Winkle was irrepressibly drunk. "What a shocking scene!" said Miss Rachael. "Dreadful, dreadful," agreed Jingle, "who was about a bottle and a half ahead of his companions"; and was now seated as close as he could contrive to Miss Rachael's side. "What a nice man!" she whispered to Mr. Tupman, whose star was sinking rapidly below the horizon.

Upstairs, awake at last after all the others had fallen asleep, the Fat Boy, the romantic moralist, the nasty story-teller who burns to shock his public, was preparing with relish for his final coup. And in the shadows behind him Fate, inexorable dictator, was busy also, maturing his counter-stroke. Mischievous morality, hopelessly over-reaching itself, is for ever devising worse harm than that which it sets out to reform.

5

Early next morning the Fat Boy brought to fruition his felonious little plan. It was the habit of old Mrs. Wardle, the timid, deaf mother of Mr. Wardle and Miss Rachael, to demand Joe's company, and the support of his arm, to help her down the garden path for half an hour's fresh air and rest in the arbour of Mr. Tupman's amorous indulgences. This was Joe's opportunity. His eyes were goggling with cruel enjoyment; the mingled yarn of his thwarted sexuality and his native spite was tangling itself in a malign confusion; he glared the old lady out of countenance, as he deposited her upon the seat.

"Missus," he shouted into her deaf ear, "I wants to make your flesh creep."

And then, with all the pomp and circumstance of a realistic novelist, he recounted the spectacle of the afternoon before. "I see him a-kissin' and a-huggin'"—"I see her a-kissin' of him again." And, having filled the poor old lady's fancy with a vision of shameless debauchery, he crunched his way up the gravel path, and left her to remorseful meditation.

Now, why did the Fat Boy behave like that? He had nothing to gain from the revelation. It was more than probable that he would be a sufferer in the reaction. The whole household would be on pins and needles. When the household was on edge, their annoyance had a way of recoiling on himself. His pleasant sleep would be interrupted by the shell-shock of his master's voice—"Joe! Drat that boy! He's asleep again." If Mr. Tupman had been intending to offer him the largess of a parting guest, he would certainly never get it now. Miss Rachael would regard him as a betrayer. No one would be grateful for knowing what they would have been happier never to know. He had everything to lose by blabbing; and yet he blabbed. Why? If he had ever heard of Rochefoucauld, he might have referred inquirers to the immortal Maxims. For no nature is so obtuse as not to savour some unholy pleasure from watching the discomfiture of its fellow-men.

"I wants to make your flesh creep." It is the secret of half the indiscretions that the human tongue is heir to. The Fat Boy, arrested in his development in so many normal directions, was yet enough of a man to feel the insidious joy of watching the eyes of his listener "bug out," like those of Huck Finn's Nigger, at the horror of his own dread story. Under his swelling waistcoat there beat the heart of the mischief-maker, the informer, the "stunt" journalist. "I wants to make your flesh creep." That was the very impulse which sent the red array of Torquemada to the Council Chamber, and still hounds the press-photographer to the door of death. The Fat Boy woke to that subtly inhuman instinct of frail humanity; and, as so often happens when the trap is set, it fell upon not one, but many, innocent and inoffensive heads.

What followed is for others in this Pickwickian Cavalcade to relate; the biographers of Jingle and Mr. Tupman must tell of the treachery of the intruder, the sudden flight, the precipitate pursuit, the running of the quarry to earth in a London inn, the bustling carnival of excitement which followed the Fat Boy's hue and cry. Of course, he was too fat to follow himself. "Now let it work. Mischief, thou art afoot," he might have cried with Antony. But he had never heard of Antony, and he had fallen asleep again. It is all very fine to talk of the sleep of the innocent. The guilty sleep just as soundly.

6

A long period was to pass, and the Pickwickians had many miles to travel before they returned to the Dingley

Dell, whose peace they had so rudely disturbed. But Mr. Wardle was not the man to nurse resentment, especially at Christmas time, and with a wedding in the bill. Mr. Trundle was to marry Miss Bella; all old friends were welcome to the halls of holly and mistletoe; and there was the Fat Boy, fatter than ever, and already, it would appear, a little chastened by experience—or was it, drugged by strong liquors?

Sam Weller was in attendance on his master, and he had never seen such obesity before, however extensive and peculiar his knowledge of human nature. He tried to chaff this lumbering portent, but he got no change out of the experiment. "You're a nice specimen of a prize boy," he began. "Now, young twenty stun." "Come along, young opium eater." But the Fat Boy had learnt the value of imperturbability. One word alone unlocked the portals of his lips. The suggestion of a drink stirred him into interest. "I likes a drop of something when it's good," he exclaimed, in a lyric sentence like a foretaste of one of Marie Lloyd's inimitable ballads. It is to be feared that the years which bring the philosophic mind had brought also to the Fat Boy a certain maudlin sentimentality, inspired by stronger spirits than his own. At the wedding feast he stood behind his master's chair in a kind of dark and gloomy joy. And when the health of the bridal couple was proposed, he was seen to be surreptitiously wiping from his eyes the tears of over-indulgence, which it would be unjust to describe as crocodiles'. The Fat Boy was growing up, and Love (of a sort) was knocking at the rusty door of his intelligence. It needed only the noise and liberty of London to set his fancy free.

The psychologist would, no doubt, trace the first

awakening of the tender passion in the Fat Boy's heavy heart, when he manifested his prurient curiosity in Mr. Tupman's amorous adventures in the arbour. Such early stirrings are commonly unpleasant—mural inscriptions in chalk, surreptitious whisperings in dim corners—every schoolmaster is familiar with the symptoms. But when adolescence settles down, like a butterfly on a flower, curiosity (the Freudian will tell you!) sinks into silence. It was even so with Mr. Wardle's Fat Boy. He had learnt, not only to go to sleep standing up, but to hold his tongue, when he was awake.

Once more Fate handed a couple of lovers over to his mercy. Just as he had caught Mr. Tupman and Miss Rachael, so the sudden opening of a door had confronted him with the spectacle of Mr. Snodgrass and Miss Emily entranced in an intimate relationship. But the days were past when he wanted to make everybody's flesh creep. Half-crowns were eagerly pressed into his palm, but he needed no bribe to secure his secrecy. "For the first and only time in his existence" he laughed aloud for sheer sympathy. Joe would never betray another lover. He was in love himself!

What malign suggestion is it that denies to the obese the right to love with chivalry and honour? Why should a fat man in love be the signal for the universal ridicule of the slim and comely? "You must show me Falstaff in love," said Queen Elizabeth; and Shakespeare, obedient to her word, sat down and wrote "The Merry Wives of Windsor." The result was the utter wreckage of Falstaff's character, the denial of all his wit, his resources, his generous manliness. Tumbled into the buck-basket, to make a Tudor holiday, the unfailing cause of humour in others expires in spirit, humourless, vapid, a drivel and a show.

The same fate closes the record of the Fat Boy in "Pickwick." With a taste beyond his training, he fixes his fancy upon a buxom wench, "nicerer" than Miss Emily, the bride elect; he chooses Mary, the housemaid, already the chosen of that triumphing Cockney, Samuel Weller. For one delicious hour, as they sit opposite one another, with a rich steak and kidney pie between them, Joe is the victim of a delusive dream. "I say, how nice you look," he whispers. And Mary throws him a smile of encouragement. "Frailty, thy name is woman." Mary is kind, only to be cruel. Her smiles are smiles of bribery. She only wants to make certain that Joe will not betray Miss Emily and Mr. Snodgrass. She need not have been afraid. Joe holds himself sealed of the tribe of true lovers. He promises; he rolls himself closer to her inviting form; he prepares to snatch a kiss. But Mary's kisses are all for Sam. She slips away and leaves him to the pie. With a sentimental light in his eyes, he helps himself to a double share, finishes it to the last crumb of nut-brown crust; and then falls fast asleep.

He wakes to the consciousness of his exhilarating secret. To keep other people's secrets he has learnt at last; but no lover ever learns how to keep his own secret. He returns to his duties in such a state of vigilance that the company are convinced he must be drunk. "I ain't drunk," he protests. Then he must be mad. "I ain't mad," he declares, "I'm sensible."

How sensible he immediately proceeds to prove by confiding his secret to the very last man in the world whom he should have chosen for his confidence.

"I say," he blurts out to Sam Weller, in a torrent of unprecedented eloquence. "What a pretty girl Mary is, isn't she? I'm so fond of her, I am."

For one moment Mr. Weller surveys his rival with a stare of contemptuous wonder. Then he seizes him by the collar, leads him to the corner, and dismisses him "with a harmless but ceremonious kick." Kicks him out of the story; kicks him out of the kingdom of romance; kicks him, finally and irretrievably, into the solitude of the obese. It may be true that fat and good humour always go together. But fatness and sentimentality, fatness and romance,—no, they are too scarce cater-cousins. They are never to be reconciled. The melody of obesity is never the food of love; the music of the fat is played upon the tongs and bones.

DR SLAMMER

By Hugh Kingsmill

XIV

I AM resolved to profit by past experience, and this time to cater for every variety of taste in Dickensian criticism. But lest in my eagerness to gratify everyone I should lay myself open to the odious suspicion of insincerity, I beg the reader to read only that section, or those sections, of my anatomy of Dr. Slammer from which his instinct tells him he will receive pleasure.

1

(This section, written to please myself, should be read only by those who are happy in my happiness.)

Blood-brother to some half-sketched giant from the pencil of Michael Angelo or howling Titan in the Prophetic Books of William Blake, Slammer, towering above the rabble of Pickwickians, stares at us for a moment, and then, dragged backward by an invisible hand, recedes into the night. Who or what is this apparition?

Slammer, as I see him, is the embodied protest of all that was good in Charles Dickens against those unholy elements in his nature which were persuading him to glorify Mr. Pickwick, instead of gibbeting him. It is obvious that Dickens's intention, in the opening pages of *Pickwick*—but here I must digress a moment. I have from time to time been rebuked for using the phrase "it is obvious," and have been assured with some heat that "it" was *not* obvious.

Dr Slammers defiance of Jingle.

All I need say on this point is that a mole is an indifferent judge of what is obvious to a lynx, and that the quality of obviousness comes into being as soon as a thing is visible to but one pair of eyes. It is obvious that Dickens's intention, in the opening pages of *Pickwick*, was, with the prevision of genius, to extirpate by ridicule the first shoots of what is nowadays called Rotarianism. Mr. Pickwick is the first Rotarian, and, had Dickens been true to his purpose, would also have been the last. Listen to him in that speech of his (Chapter I) which gropes in the rotund oratory of the age of Daniel O'Connell towards the ideal since crisply enshrined in "Service not Self"—"He (Mr. Pickwick) would not deny that he was influenced by human passions, and human feelings (cheers)—possibly by human weaknesses—(loud cries of 'No'); but this he would say that if ever the fire of self-importance broke out in his bosom, the desire to benefit the human race in preference, effectually quenched it." There speaks the real Pickwick, the smoothest produce broker on 'Change, the man who, in conjunction with the Cheeryble Brothers, engineered the coconut boom of '26, and, by God's Providence, got out in the nick of time.

It is obvious from a hundred indications, which will no doubt be fully catalogued elsewhere in this volume, that Dickens's original intention was to show Mr. Pickwick touring the country in search of profitable investments in real estate. He took Tupman with him because Tupman was useful in negotiations where Mr. Pickwick preferred not to appear in person. Married to a woman of great physical strength and ungovernable jealousy, Tupman had once been extricated by Mr. Pickwick from a very unsavoury scrape, and thereafter their business relations were of the most intimate. Snodgrass and Winkle, young and wealthy, accompanied Mr. Pickwick because they hoped, under his direction, to recoup their losses over coconut.

I have no space to go into the reasons which led Dickens, almost at once, to depart from his original design. Inherent in his divided nature, these reasons are fully and—may I add?—tenderly set forth in a recent brochure from my pen. Here I am simply concerned to point out that the clash at Rochester between Slammer and the Pickwickians, though superficially motivated by Slammer's chagrin at the conduct of Jingle, was really the last desperate explosion of Dickens, the genius, against the impostor whom Dickens, the public entertainer, had taken under his protection. It is the genius, in the persons of Dr. Slammer, Dr. Payne, and Lieutenant Tappleton, who withdraws from the scene, but the honours of the conflict go with him. Has Rotarian heroism, the essence of which consists in correct timing, ever been more blisteringly illustrated than in this paragraph? I italicise the key sentences. "Rising rage and extreme bewilderment had swelled the noble breast of Mr. Pickwick, almost to the bursting of his waistcoat, during the delivery of the above defiance. *He stood transfixed to the spot, gazing on vacancy. The closing of the door recalled him to himself.* He rushed forward with fury in his looks, and fire in his eye. His hand was upon the lock of the door; in another instant it would have been upon the throat of Dr. Payne of the Forty-third, had not Mr. Snodgrass seized his revered leader by the coat tail and dragged him backwards."

2

(This section should prove of absorbing interest to lovers of the Master. Based on hitherto unpublished information about the person from whom Dickens drew Dr. Slammer, it is a model of biographical exactitude combined with good taste and charity, and the whole is pervaded with a certain wistful charm.)

It was my great good fortune, when a small boy aged some nine summers, to enjoy the privilege of an acquaintance with the daughter of the medical officer who served Charles Dickens as model for the peppery but good-hearted Dr. Slammer, whose *rencontre* with Jingle and subsequent cross-purposes *vis-à-vis* of the unmartial Mr. Winkle furnish one of the brightest episodes in the immortal Odyssey of Mr. Pickwick. The lady in question was a Miss Amy Parkes, who at the period of our acquaintanceship, in the autumn of 1899, had attained the ripe age of ninety-two. Yet were her faculties still undimmed, and she manifested a great delight, not perhaps untinged with amusement, at my absorption in the novels of the Master. Many an hour did we spend in pleasant chat about those imperishable creations who to her, in the sunset of her day, as to me in the dawning of mine, were more real than the persons of the so-called real world. Her own favourite was Miss Betsy Trotwood, and I have sometimes ventured to surmise that her sympathy with that redoubtable lady was based on a certain similarity of temperament. But this is merely conjecture. The venue of our talks was, of all appropriate places, the Leather Bottle at Cobham, whither my parents had taken me to recuperate after a bout of

measles, and I sometimes fancied that the stout shade of
Mr. Tracy Tupman presided over our conferences. Yet
was it noticeable even to my childish apprehensions that
Miss Parkes manifested a certain reserve whenever our talk
veered in the direction of the Pickwick Papers, and, one
day, summoning up my courage, for a very decided awe
was mingled with my affection, I ventured to inquire the
reason for her seeming coldness towards that incomparable
masterpiece. Rearranging her shawl with a slight air of
agitation, she replied—"My dear child, I really ought to
be cross with Mr. Dickens. He was not very kind about
Papa. No one living knows it, and I never mention it, but
you are so young. Will you promise me, Hugh, to keep it
a secret? At least while I still live. Sometimes I fancy that
my time will not be long now." Her voice quavered, but
as I swore myself to secrecy, in a childish treble which
drew a smile to her lips, she resumed her self-possession,
and continued. "Papa was born in 1781. Isn't that a long
time ago? He was a medical officer in the army during the
wars against the Corsican usurper, and was foremost after
the battle of Waterloo in succouring the victims of that
glorious day. My dear Mama and he were married in 1806,
and after the peace they settled in Chatham, at Number
Two, Ordnance Terrace. A few doors away lived the
parents of Charles Dickens, and though they were very
nice and good people they were not quite—you know.
Papa and Mama were always very friendly towards them,
but social distinctions were stricter in those days, and so
Mr. and Mrs. John Dickens—that was their name—were
not on visiting terms with Papa and Mama, and I am afraid
that little Charles, who was a very bright and precocious
child, resented this. He used to make faces at Papa in the

street, and one day Papa, who was kindness itself, lost his temper and gave Charles a sound smacking!" The old lady laughed merrily as she spoke. "Fancy CHARLES DICKENS being smacked! But, of course, no one realised then that he was different from any other little boy who hadn't learnt reverence for his elders and betters. And I am sure he deserved it." Her lips tightened, and for a moment the dear old lady looked really formidable. "After that," she resumed, "Charles kept out of Papa's way. But he never forgot. I am afraid there was something a little hard in his nature, or perhaps it was only that he was more sensitive than others. And so, you see, he put Papa into that book. Everyone knew that Dr. Slammer was meant for Papa, because Papa was in the 79th, and Dr. Slammer was in the 97th, which is the same number the other way about. And Papa *was* short, and perhaps a little inclined to *embonpoint*, and he was the life and soul of every party, just like Dr. Slammer. But he would never have *dreamed* of paying attentions to a common little woman like that Mrs. Budger, even after Mama had passed away, and Mama was still with us when that book was written. Papa was *devoted* to Mama, and never looked at anyone else, and after she had passed away he married her greatest friend. Mama was dreadfully hurt about Mrs. Budger, but Papa was crosser because Mr. Dickens described him as fat, and he wasn't *really* fat, though perhaps a little inclined to *embonpoint*."

Such, as nearly as possible in the very words which she employed, was the story the old lady told me. The impression it made on me deepened as I grew older, and often in later years, when I have reflected upon it, it has seemed to me to illustrate in a very striking manner the unforeseen, and sometimes unfortunate, results produced by the strange thing we call genius. What would Charles Dickens, kindliest of men, have felt, had he known that in the carefree exercise of his matchless humour he had given pain to these simple souls? Yet it was so.

3

(This section may be read with perfect confidence by those to whom the preceding section has given satisfaction. It is of a topographical nature.)

Of all the fascinating evenings which I spent in the company of my late lamented friend, and fervent fellow-Dickensian, Mr. Arthur Wimpole, the most memorable was that in which he succeeded in convincing me that it was in the coffee-room of the Bull, not in a private sitting-room of that hostelry, that Mr. Pickwick received Dr. Slammer and his friends, and was prevented only by the timely intervention of Mr. Snodgrass from falling upon them single-handed.

How well I remember the twinkle in his eye when, in answer to the above assertion, I exclaimed—"But Mr. Pickwick engaged a private sitting-room. I remember the very words—'A private sitting-room having been engaged, bedrooms inspected, and . . .'"

Wimpole held up his hand. "My dear Kingsmill," he said, "your memory is, as always, infallible. But what about Jingle?" I must have looked my bewilderment, for he continued in that slow, charming way of his—"When Mr. Pickwick engaged that sitting-room, he had in mind a place to which he could retreat with his friends, Tupman,

Winkle, and Snodgrass. Remember, Mr. Pickwick was a
gentleman. Jingle intrigued him, but he didn't want Jingle
right on top of him. True, he had just asked him to dinner.
That was the friendly thing to do, for Jingle wasn't—
apparently—putting up at the Bull. You may recall that
after accepting Mr. Pickwick's invitation, Jingle walked
off and vanished up the High Street. Now how do you
think Mr. Pickwick felt when he learnt the next morning
that Jingle had spent the night in Snodgrass's bed, with
Snodgrass perched beside him on three rickety chairs?"

"My dear Wimpole!"

"Mind you, I'm going a little beyond my book at this
point. I don't *know* that Jingle turned Snodgrass out of his
own bed. But I am perfectly clear that he spent the night
at the Bull."

"And what, if I may ask, is your authority for this bold
statement?"

"Slammer. Don't you remember? Come now!"

"Oh, you mean when he says to Jingle—'You are
stopping in this house, sir . . . you shall hear from me in
the morning, sir.' But, hang it, Wimpole, that's not
evidence. How the deuce could Slammer know where
Jingle was stopping?"

"And why the deuce should he pretend to know if he
didn't? He wasn't that type. There was no finesse about
Dr. Slammer! I think we may pretty safely conclude that
he'd been interviewing one of the chambermaids while
Tupman was hopping round with Mrs. Budger, and that
Jingle had told the girl he'd be turning in with Snodgrass
for the night, and would move into another room when
the hotel had emptied itself after the ball."

"Plausible, Wimpole, I admit. Plausible. And yet—and

yet. Granted that Jingle *may* have taken up his quarters in the Bull, granted that Mr. Pickwick, unable to shake him off, *may* have preferred to entertain him in the coffee-room, and so have virtually abandoned the use of his private sitting-room, I confess that I would like more than merely presumptive evidence."

"What about Dismal Jimmy, eh?"

"The strolling actor who turns up suddenly under Jingle's wing?"

"Precisely. Are you going to tell me that Mr. Pickwick, a dignified English gentleman, wasn't going to draw the line at having his private quarters invaded by Jingle *and* Dismal Jimmy?"

"It's a strong point, Wimpole, and yet for the life of me——"

"You don't think it conclusive. You're right. It didn't quite settle the matter for me either. So—" his eyes lit up, and he looked triumphantly across at me—"So I went down to the Bull, and what do you think I found?" He rubbed his hands with an indescribable expression of gratification. "You know the Bull as well as I do, Kingsmill. Ever noticed the coffee-room door?"

"Not particularly, I am ashamed to confess."

"Remember, it hasn't been touched since Dickens's day, nor have any of the doors upstairs."

"Well?" I was all impatience.

Wimpole leant forward, and, wagging his forefinger at me, said in a measured voice—"Every door in the house has the ordinary door handle—they were put in during the Regency—*except* the coffee-room. It has—and always has had—a latch, or lock, as they used to call it. Or *lock*." He leant back, and smiled at me with supreme complacence.

"Well, what then?"

"Where's your memory, Kingsmill, where's your memory? 'The closing of the door recalled him to himself. He rushed forward with fury in his looks, and fire in his eye. His hand was upon the'—Wimpole's voice sank to a whisper—'*lock of the door*.' "

"Great!" I cried. "Great! You must put it on paper, you *must*. Wimpole, when are we to have the book on Dickens which only you can give us? When are you going to rescue him from the clutches of the debunkers and the psycho-analysers?" "*À quoi sert-il?*" he murmured, with a melancholy smile. "The Master is there for all to read. Let each man read him by his own private light—or darkness." He shrugged his shoulders.

4

(In this section a post-war novelist of my acquaintance sends me some jottings on Slammer and others. It is a section which should make a very definite appeal to those who have not found what they were looking for in the previous two sections.)

DEAR KINGSMILL,—

I am highly intrigued by your suggestion that I should rewrite *The Pickwick Papers* before beginning my next book. It ought to give me just the kind of rest I need. I've been running through it, and there are obvious possibilities. The man can turn up the stuff, though he hasn't the vaguest idea what to make of it when it's there in front of him. Look at the way he's foozled Slammer, the one

character in the book that it was absolutely *fatal* to foozle.
Have you seen Hugo Koenigsmuehle on the English
Œdipus? Get it, if you haven't. It's just been translated.
H. K.'s idea is that most Englishmen haven't got the
normal Œdipus—marrying one's mother and murdering
one's father—but have a modification of it in the form of a
desire to murder both parents. Social and other inhibitions
blocking this desire, you get the English restlessness, love
of travel, exploration, etc. Hence the British Empire. It
looks water-tight to me, and Slammer fits into it very
nicely—army surgeon, service in India, and so forth,
loathes the home-staying type (Pickwick has an obvious
mother-fixation. So, I think, has Winkle. Jingle's betwixt
and between). And Slammer's affair with the Budger
crone goes beautifully with H. K.'s theory of a reversion
to the normal Œdipus after forty. Of course I take my
psycho-analysis with a pinch of salt. But it helps.

That's useful, what you tell me about Dickens and Maria
Beadnell (what *delicious* names those dear people had!
Why don't we revive them?). I agree, of course, that
Martha Bardell chasing Pickwick is a revenge-inversion,
to soothe the sting of the Beadnell business. By switching
it back again, with Pickwick after Martha and Slammer
cutting in and getting away with M. B., I have my main
theme sitting pretty, and can use as much or as little of the
junk with which Dickens clutters up the book as I find
convenient. I think I'll keep the Wellers. Sam has the
makings of a pretty blackmailer. He ought to find Slammer
a goldmine when the old boy's trying to cut loose from
the Budger; and Tony will come in on the rough stuff
when Slammer shows his teeth. And there ought to be
some pickings for Sam during the house-warming at

Wardle's. How that man Dickens throws his chances away !
When there's nothing else offering, Sam can keep in form
by double-crossing Pickwick. Yes, I'll use Sam.

All this is hopelessly provisional, but let me have your
ideas on it.

Yours ever,

T. H.

P.S. Of course I shall keep the original atmosphere.

P.P.S. It has just dawned on me that I needn't discard
the Fat Boy if I pare him to normal dimensions. At his
present weight he is simply meaningless.

5

(Conscious that this anatomy of Dr. Slammer was un-
finished, but uncertain whose voice I was still waiting to
hear, I fell into a profound muse, during which I seemed
to be transported to a warm and misty interior where dim
murmurs of "minesaguinness" and "bassforme" filled the
air, until at last out of the babble a voice took shape, and
a vast cloudy form, and these words became audible to
me.)

". . . If I have heard you aright, and your efforts to be
articulate have certainly deserved success, and I heartily hope
have also commanded it, I say, if I have heard you aright,
and Mr. Kingsmill is in sober truth—if you will pardon
the expression—writing on Dr. Slammer, then all I need
say, but by no means all I intend to say, is that Mr. Pickwick is avenged—to say nothing of Mr. Winkle, for that
goes without saying, and to say nothing of Jingle, because

in this connection and on this occasion, and in this connection alone, and on this occasion alone, there is nothing to be said about Jingle. With the possible exception of every other character in the novels of Charles Dickens, there is no single character in the novels of Charles Dickens about whom Mr. Kingsmill is more certain to go wrong, and therefore less certain to go right, than the character whom I shall call, for the sake of convenience no less than in the interests of a perhaps pedantic accuracy, Dr. Slammer. I say nothing against Mr. Kingsmill, who for all I know to the contrary may be the life and soul—I withdraw the odious expression—the psyche and the subconscious of every psycho-pathological clinic between Vienna and Berlin. Mr. Kingsmill may be, and I dare say is, the best of fellows, with the correct number of repressions, complexes and inhibitions, all accurately ticketed and in good running order. But—yes, mine is a Guinness. And by the way what a splendidly shattering and satisfying sound those words have! If Shakespeare were alive to-day, as he unquestionably would be had he not been killed by his commentators, he could not find, and would be much too sensible to attempt to find, any more royal and ringing opening to a sonnet than that which has just fallen from my—alas, only momentarily inspired— lips . . .

> Mine is a Guinness. Let no baser word
> Profane the lips by Guinness once bedewed. . . .

We were talking about Mr. Kingsmill, a strange thing to do. I do not propose to tax your memory by inquiring how we came upon this recondite theme. On the contrary I shall earn your gratitude, even at the risk of exposing myself to the disgusting imputation of tact, by returning to our muttons—a quaint old-world phrase which is doubtless more familiar to your ears in its modern form of returning to our triturated parsnips. There are roughly two thousand three hundred and forty-six ways in which the modern world is certain to go wrong about Dr. Slammer, and if I were not unfortunately as old as the night is still fortunately young, I should examine as many of these ways as your capacity for sleeping while others talk would allow me to; a capacity, I may remark in passing, which I am beginning to suspect that I have very seriously under-estimated. But in the circumstances I shall content myself with the simple observation that the modern world cannot understand the relations between the retired merchant, Mr. Pickwick, and the anything but retiring army surgeon, Dr. Slammer, because the modern world has not yet arrived at even a glimmering of the truth that opposites are not necessarily, if indeed they ever are, mutually exclusive. The North and South Poles are opposites, but they would get on uncommonly badly without each other. Mr. Pickwick and Dr. Slammer were opposites, and if you should reply, with the lightning quickness which distinguished you earlier in the evening, that they got on uncommonly badly *with* each other, I have only to retort that so would the North and South Poles, if in a mood of pardonable curiosity or fit of comprehensible impatience they arranged to meet at the Equator. Nevertheless, they are indispensable to each other, exactly as Mr. Pickwick and Dr. Slammer were indispensable to each other. In the modern world the soldier has been transformed into a mechanic who is paralysed by his machine, and the merchant into the cog of a machine which won't work. If ever—as, please God, it may—the England of Charles Dickens shall return, it will be between the poles of Dr. Slammer and Mr. Pickwick that it will revolve again, between the public servant who is always too busy to settle down and the private trader who is never too busy to settle up. It is the greatest of the many great glories of Charles Dickens that he was able to imagine Dr. Slammer as well as Mr. Pickwick. It was perhaps not the least of his mistakes that he brought them together.

DINGLEY DELL
v.
ALL-MUGGLETON
CRICKET MATCH
By A. G. Macdonell

XV

IT was a fortunate circumstance that, on the occasion of the grand match between the cricket team of the corporate town of Muggleton and the representatives of the hamlet of Dingley Dell, there should have been present on the ground, by pure chance, at least one person who understood the game of the cricket both in its subtleties and in its noble essentials. For, with the exception of this one fortuitous spectator, and possibly, just possibly, one other, there does not seem to have been anyone else on the Muggleton ground that day, either bowler or batsman, umpire, captain, fieldsman, or on-looker, who understood more than the rudiments of the pastime. I say it is just possible that there was one other who may have appreciated the finer points, at any rate of village cricket, and, as he can be discussed and dismissed in a moment, I will get him out of the way without more ado.

Mr. Snodgrass, in order to make conversation at the breakfast-table after the unfortunate shooting-accident to Mr. Tupman—and making conversation at that table after that accident was no light matter, for Mr. Pickwick, with doubt and distrust exhibited in his countenance, was silent and reserved—inquired of Mr. Wardle whether he was a cricketer.

"I was once upon a time," replied the host; "but I have given it up now. I subscribe to the club here, but I don't play."

The Cricket Match.
(R.W. Buss – Suppressed Plate)

Now it cannot be pure chance that Mr. Wardle should have compressed into four short sentences the whole duty of the country landlord towards the sport of his tenantry and of his farmering neighbours. Mr. Wardle must have known, instinctively, through centuries of inherited squiredom, that every squire must have a legendary fame for prodigious feats on the pitches of long-ago, must on no account hazard that fame among a generation that was unborn when he was laying on the wood, and must subscribe to the Club.

Let us allow, then, to Mr. Wardle at least a knowledge of rural etiquette, and also a legendary fame. For whenever a squire is known to have been a cricketer in the days before the memory of all except a few greybeards, it is an axiom that he was an exceptionally fine player.

But the real expert upon the Muggletonian ground was, of course, Mr. Alfred Jingle. Mr. Jingle had a remarkably wide experience of cricket. Not only had he played the game, on his own admission, some thousands of times, but he appears to have been many years ahead of Lord Hawke in popularising the game in the West Indies. He also was responsible for the introduction of several interesting innovations into the rules, especially of the single-wicket game, a variation of cricket which has been unhappily allowed to sink into comparative desuetude in our times. For instance, it was Mr. Jingle who introduced the idea of starting a match at the cool hour of 7 a.m., an example which, if it had been followed during that unfortunate season not so long ago when some very distinguished players discovered, apparently for the first time, that cricket is played with a hard ball, might have averted much imperial bad temper.

It was Mr. Jingle, again, who first organised relays of fieldsmen—six at a time—to replace casualties. It is a pity that this magnificent conception should have been whittled down in a modern cricket to the provision of an occasional substitute, but I have no doubt in my own mind that it has been directly responsible for some of the manlier aspects of American football, a game in which the quick succeed to the dead in bewildering succession. Nor was Mr. Jingle parochially-minded. There was no narrow snobbery about him. Realising, long before his time, the immense value of organised games in welding together this heritage of ours into a happy empire, Mr. Jingle encouraged the West Indian natives not only to play cricket, but even to participate in matches with the ruling classes, including Colonel Sahibs, and it is hardly an exaggeration to say that Constantine and Headley are spiritual descendants of that great-hearted Quanko Samba who literally bowled himself to death. As for Mr. Jingle's own personal skill, I have searched all the records in vain for a score which exceeds his famous West Indian record of five hundred and seventy runs in one completed innings, mostly compiled with a seriously-blistered bat, and so far as I know it still holds the field for the single-wicket game. Indeed, it held the field for all classes of cricket including Matches against Odds, Smokers *v.* Non-Smokers, and Ladies *v.* Gentlemen (with broomsticks), until it was finally surpassed in 1899 by A. E. J. Collins at Clifton College with his 628 not out for Clarke's House *v.* North Town.

This, then, was the redoubtable cricketer who happened, by a lucky chance, to be present at the Muggleton ground on the day of the grand match.

Of course, from the outset Mr. Jingle had no illusions about the class of performance he was about to witness. It was not exactly the sort of thing he was accustomed to, but there is something in the very soul of cricket which creates an atmosphere of gentle, genial tolerance, and the greatest of players can be happy upon the humblest of greens. Thus Mr. Jingle saw at a glance that this was to be no desperate encounter such as the match between the Parish of Farnham (with Felix given) and All-England, but an occasion of social festivity regardless of the final markings of the scorers. Unerringly, therefore, he cast his eye over the luncheon arrangements (he had previously done the same office for the dinner to be held at the Blue Lion after the match), knowing well that if they were defective the social basis of the match would disintegrate. A gloom has been cast over more than one pleasant game by the presence of beef but absence of mustard, or vice versa. But here everything was in order, with rounds of the one and cartloads of the other, and the rigour of the play and the appearance of the players were at once relegated in his mind to a status of minor importance. The latter, indeed, must have appeared unusual to an experienced eye. The holder of the single-wicket record of the Empire could seldom have played his big matches against opponents who looked like amateur-stonemasons, or who were so prodigiously stout that they looked like gigantic rolls of flannel elevated on a couple of inflated pillow-cases. Nevertheless Mr. Jingle's comments were wise and illuminating. He first summed up the game itself in six profound words. "Capital game"—for those who have the art to play it as a game of skill; "Smart sport," even for those who, sons of a sporting race, are compelled by the tenuity of their resources to look like amateur stone-masons; and, because your true cricketer's charity is inexhaustible, there are two words of kindly encouragement for those who look like the gigantic rolls of flannel and have neither skill at the game nor smartness at the sport, "Fine exercise."

From this brilliant, generous, and epigrammatic description of the pastime, Mr. Jingle at once turns to the players. He has only just formed their acquaintance; he feels instinctively that by his standards they are not expert cricketers; their clothes are unlike the clothes of Lord's. But they are cricketers and that is enough for him. "Splendid fellows—glorious," he cries, and one feels that any man, "be he ne'er so vile," so long as he is a devotee of cricket, is to Mr. Jingle a splendid and glorious fellow.

It need hardly be supposed that the one-sided nature of the grand match escaped such an expert eye. Mr. Jingle had not yet visited Dingley Dell, but he was not likely to be misled into thinking that it was a corporate town like its opponent, with mayor, burgesses, and freemen, taking a zealous part in high affairs, now petitioning the High Court of Parliament against the continuance of this, now against any interference with that, possessing corn-factors and fire-agencies, and, although sometimes addicted to torpor, at others nevertheless holding the strongest views on Simony and Sunday-trading. Mr. Jingle was hardly such a simpleton as to believe any such thing, and it is more than likely that he admired the Davidian courage of the tiny hamlet as much as he must have secretly deplored the slightly—shall we say—unsporting action of Muggleton in still further weighting the scales against its tiny adversary by recruiting its forces not only from the corporate town proper, but from the outlying districts, suburbs, and surrounding farms as well. (At least, that is how I read the circumstance that the team was called, not simply Muggleton, but All-Muggleton.)

But whatever Mr. Jingle felt on these matters, as on certain others that arose during the course of the match, he very wisely held his peace.

The spin was made for choice of innings, and Fortune, favouring as usual the big battalions, came down on the side of All-Muggleton, who very naturally elected to bat first. The wicket was hard, for there had been no rain for some time, and the Muggletonians, though mere townees, were sufficiently versed in weather lore to know that the sun, darting his bright beams since early morning, would long since have dried up the dew, which otherwise, had it still been glistening on every leaf as it trembled in the gentle air, might have made the fast bowling fly awkwardly.

The opening pair of batsmen were a Mr. Podder, known throughout the entire district as a pretty warm man in anything connected with Real Estate, and a Mr. Dumkins, both citizens born and bred of the town. And before we go any further, a word about this latter gentleman might not be out of place. Mr. Dumkins was a remarkable character. Still young enough to be one of the two best batsmen in the town, he was old enough to be regarded by his fellow-citizens as an authentic village, or rather town, Hampden. No generous cause ever appealed to him in vain; no defence of liberty, right, or privilege ever found Mr. Dumkins shirking from the barricades; and once he had set his hand to a task, he carried it through to the end with such inflexible determination that the word passed into general currency, and Dumkins for Determination became a famous tag. There were many citizens of Muggleton who could have told you that in their hour of misgiving and despair, the name of Dumkins, or, better still, a word of encouragement from his lips, had given them fresh inspiration and fire with which to resume the fight. I make no doubt whatever that five years after this cricket-match, Mr. Dumkins was carrying the torch of Reform with all the bulldog tenacity with which he carried his bat.

This, then, was the redoubtable pair which made its way to the wickets, and the grand match began.

It was fortunate indeed that the famous stranger was so imbued with the broad charity of cricket, for outwardly he showed no sort of astonishment at the proceedings which now unrolled themselves before him.

No sooner had the All-Muggleton pair taken up their positions at the wickets, than the Dingley Dell captain issued the strangest instructions. For he deputed his champion player, a Mr. Luffey, to bowl to Mr. Dumkins, and his second bowler, a Mr. Struggles, to bowl to Mr. Podder. Now this can only mean that the Dingley Dellers were not accustomed to deliver the ball in sequences of four, five, six, or even eight balls from the same end (each sequence forming what is called an "over"), and that, furthermore, they did not anticipate that their opponents would score in anything but twos, fours, or sixes. For imagine the confusion that would ensue if a stroke was played by which an odd number of runs was notched. If Podder scored a single off Struggles, the run would bring him to the wicket that faced Luffey. But Luffey's task was to bowl to Dumkins. Luffey would, therefore, have to cross over and change places with Struggles. But, then, whose turn would it be to bowl? This was confusion bad enough at the very beginning. Worse was to follow. The umpires, whether they were vague about their duties or whether they were bewildered by the bowling tactics of the Dingley Dellers, instead of taking post one at the bowler's end and the other at square-leg, both stood behind the wickets.

Now Mr. Jingle, veteran of thousands of matches, knew as well as his neighbour that an umpire behind the wickets at the bowler's end is admirably placed for a clear view of the proceedings over which he is to preside, but that an umpire standing behind the wickets at the batsman's end is not only in grave physical danger, but must seriously incommode the wicket-keeper in the execution of his duties. Mr. Jingle, to his great credit, preferred to make no comment upon these arrangements, but rather to concentrate, as a connoisseur should, upon the virtuosity of the play itself.

The fieldsmen were stationed at their several posts, the scorers sat alertly with knife and stick in one of the two marquees, the best place in the whole field, and Mr. Luffey polished the ball ominously against his right eyelid. Then, without waiting for the umpire at the bowler's wicket to open the match with his ceremonious "Play!" Mr. Luffey suddenly performed that office himself and simultaneously delivered a fast, dead-straight yorker or low full-pitch—the point will be argued in a moment— as nasty a ball as any batsman could hope for at the very beginning of an innings. I must hasten to add that I am not for one moment ascribing to Mr. Luffey's account any sort of sharp practice in this explosive opening. I am merely recording the facts. In any case it mattered little either way so far as the actual game was concerned, for Mr. Dumkins, wary and alert, was no more to be caught napping by a cricket-ball than by an illegal blocking of a right-of-way or the enclosure of a piece of common land.

Now as to that first ball. It was fast and straight, and Mr. Dumkins was only able to hit it with the very end of his bat. That sounds as if it must have been a yorker. On the other hand, the ball flew off ·the bat upwards and travelled for a considerable distance, an occurrence that is extremely rare off a yorker, if not almost unprecedented. It is more likely, then, that the ball was a low full-pitch, and that Mr. Dumkins mishit it off the end of his bat over the heads of the slips—the slips being, I think, the only group of fieldsmen which fits the narrative. For it will be observed that the ball flew over the heads of more than one man, and that it was moving so fast that they had not time to spring up from their professional crouch in order to intercept it. (I dismiss with scorn the suggestion that Mr. Luffey was bowling to a leg-side field, with four short-legs clustering round the batsman's elbow, the only other formation which would fit the text.) Let us conclude, therefore, that the stroke was a snick over the slips which a little more activity by those gentlemen might well have converted into a catch, and that Mr. Dumkins was very lucky not to be out first ball, either clean-bowled or caught. Two runs were notched by this indifferent shot, and the prudent batsmen were in no way flustered by the conflicting shouts and useless advice of their supporters.

A few minutes later it was the turn of Mr. Struggles to try to succeed where all other neighbouring bowlers had failed that year, and bring to an end the remarkable series of not-out innings wherewith Mr. Podder had garnished the laurels of himself and of Muggleton's season. For it is clear that when a batsman is chronicled in the description of a match as "hitherto unconquered" before he has received so much as a single ball, the phrase can only refer to the earlier matches of the year (for I think we may dismiss as pedantry the suggestion that the chronicler contemplated that Mr. Podder might be run out off the first ball that Mr. Dumkins received. Indeed it is more than pedantry. It is out of character. The champion of liberal causes would never allow a partner to be involved in a catastrophe which he himself did not share, nor would the cautious man of property have accepted such a risk).

Mr. Struggles advanced to the attack, and soon found that Mr. Podder was a very irritating customer. It was not that he was especially dexterous as a batsman. Quite the reverse. But he had developed to an extraordinary degree of efficacy the peculiarly unorthodox style which is almost universal upon the village grounds of to-day. That is to say, whenever a ball was bowled to him about which he was doubtful—or as the modern phrase has it, by which he was caught in two minds—he blocked it, either by chopping sharply down upon it, I imagine, or simply by not moving his bat at all. On the other hand, when Mr. Struggles tempted him with a bad ball, with a long-hop, perhaps, for a snick to the wicket-keeper, or with a full-pitch to leg for a catch on the boundary, Mr. Podder's repertory of strokes was so limited that, try as he might, he could not get his bat close enough to the ball even to snick it. But when it came to a good ball, a ball turning, let us suppose, sharply from the off-stump to the leg-stump or one that swung outwards and late, Mr. Podder took it and sent it flying to all parts of the field. We all know those batsmen who send the good balls flying to all parts of the field. On the offside, the execution is done with the edge of the bat, mostly through the slips and past third-man, with an occasional hit that pitches to the right of cover-point's right hand and spins very suddenly and obliquely across his front and past his left hand. On the leg-side, the deadly work is pursued by converting the bat into a scythe and sweeping every ball round to leg, with the right knee on the ground. Many a match has been won or lost in a very few minutes by a batsman of this calibre, and Mr. Podder, hitherto unconquered throughout the season, mind you, was no mean exponent of this style.

Nor was this all that the bowlers had to contend with. The ground-fielding was slovenly and at least one (not counting the possible chance off the first ball of the day) comparatively simple catch was missed. The ball was travelling hard, it is true, but it was head-high and straight to the fieldsman, and the bowler was entitled to expect that the fieldsman at least would get a hand to it. Instead of which he never even touched it, and he thoroughly deserved the indignant "Now, butterfingers," with which the august spectator stigmatised his incompetence.

For although Mr. Jingle had courteously refrained from commenting upon some of the arrangements and strategy of the rustic play, he did not feel himself similarly debarred from a discussion of the points of the game as it proceeded. (This habit of maintaining a running commentary upon a cricket-match in progress is very popular, I understand, in the outlying portions of our Empire, and it is certain that Mr. Jingle must have picked it up in the Antilles.)

Hence his exclamation of "Now, butterfingers" when the slim fieldsman allowed the catch to strike him on the nose and bound pleasantly off with redoubled violence. But although Mr. Jingle's high standards did not allow him to pass unblamed bad attempts to catch the ball or failures to stop it, still less did his generous nature allow him to pass unpraised any piece of work which might even remotely be described as a good stroke, and his applause rang out frequently. Needless to say, his obvious satisfaction and approval on these latter occasions were highly gratifying to the parties concerned, coming as they did from such an excellent judge.

Meanwhile Mr. Dumkins and Mr. Podder were laying on vigorously, and the half-century had been passed for the first wicket, in spite of numerous changes of bowling, before the partnership was broken. Dumkins was the first to go, a catch being held at last, and then, shortly afterwards, a belated triumph fell to the Dingley Dell bowlers when the colours of the redoubtable Podder were hauled down on appeal to the umpire. For the man of property, flown with success, sprang out of his crease at a ball, probably one of Struggles's worst, missed it as usual, and was stumped.

But although the score was now fifty-four for two wickets, which is vastly better for the fielding-side than fifty for no wickets, it is not surprising that the Dingley Dellers wore a somewhat blank expression on their faces.[1] Any score over fifty is a good score on a village ground for a whole team, and there were still eight more All-

---

[1] By a curious error or misunderstanding, the chronicler records that at this point in the match the Dingley Dellers had failed to score. They had, of course, not yet batted.

Muggletons to be disposed of. Messrs. Luffey and Struggles refused to give up hope, and fought on eagerly and enthusiastically. But the advantage was too great to be recovered. Dingley Dell batted, were compelled to follow on, and, although they saved the innings defeat, nevertheless were beaten by a handsome margin very early in the fourth innings. But there is small doubt that the losers were consoled, as the winners were delighted, by Mr. Jingle's final verdict, "Capital game—well played." Then, as if to fill their cup to overflowing, the great and generous man added—perhaps with a silent prayer to Heaven for forgiveness: "Some strokes admirable."

The grand match was over. Stumps were drawn. The company straggled off in the evening sun to the Blue Lion Inn, where they sat down to a hearty cold supper, with the usual accompaniments of such occasions, speeches, toasts, and songs.

The party broke up at a late hour, and another cricket-match had gone to join the shades.

One last word. So little did Mr. Pickwick understand what was going forward on the green at Muggleton, that, many months later, when he befriended Mr. Alfred Jingle and paid his passage back to the West Indies, he actually advised him to give up cricket altogether. Mr. Jingle, although overcome with emotion at the moment, retained sufficient presence of mind to make no promises, and I have no doubt that his anxiety to earn money to repay the fifty pounds and more which Mr. Pickwick had laid out on his behalf was stronger than his regard for his benefactor's advice, and that, immediately on landing at Demerara, he turned professional.

THE SMALLEST FRY
By James Agate

XVI

LIKE a bolt from the Brighton blue came this strange telegram: "Will you do Minor Characters Pickwick Bertie." Now I had heard of Burlington Bertie but never of Pickwick Bertie, and for a space I was befogged. Three times back and forth along that Georgian and somehow Dickensian front which we shall presently see no more, and I had solved the mystery. Bertie was Bertie van Thal, and B. van T., in turn, was Chapman and Hall, and Chapman and Hall were Dickens's original publishers, and this is the centenary of *Pickwick*, and the invitation had to do with a symposium. I wired back: "There are No Minor Characters in Pickwick James" and went to lunch, vastly pleased at having got so much truth into such small compass.

What is a major character and what is a minor one? I shall not go into this, since that way the dullest of literary essays lies. Leaving *Pickwick* aside for a moment, let me ask how many major characters there are in, for example, *Hamlet*. I can think of only two—Hamlet and his mother. Of minor-major characters I can think of four—the King, Ophelia, Laertes, Polonius. Among the major-minor characters I would include Horatio, the Player King, and the First Gravedigger. Among minor characters I would rank Osric the water-fly and Fortinbras the water-buffalo. And I am not at all sure that there shouldn't be a sub-minor category to include Marcellus, Rosencrantz, Guildenstern. These are the play's inconsiderable fry, and what Voltimand says to Cornelius was never, of course, evidence!

The Card Room at Bath.

Something of the same dividuppableness appertains to *Pickwick*. My working edition contains a list of the characters, and to my amazement all the characters included are major characters. Will it be believed that there is no mention in this list of Joseph Smiggers, Esq., P.V.P.M.P.C., who "felt it his imperative duty to demand of the honourable gentleman, whether he had used the expression which had just escaped him in a common sense"? Nor is there mention of Mr. Blotton, who "was bound to acknowledge that, personally, he entertained the highest regard and esteem for the honourable gentleman; he had merely considered him a humbug in a Pickwickian point of view." This is not, as so many have wrongly assumed, Mr. Blotton's unique appearance, for whereas Mr. Smiggers flashes meteor-like across the Pickwickian sky, Mr. Blotton makes cometary return. It was Blotton and no other who in connection with Cobham's antique stone "wrote a pamphlet, addressed to the seventeen learned societies, native and foreign, containing a repetition of the statement he had already made, and rather more than half intimating his opinion that the seventeen learned societies were so many 'humbugs.'" Blotton, we can clearly see, is a man with an *idée fixe*. Yes, Blotton is a personage, while it is conceivable that Smiggers is merely a person. However this may be, I feel that I know them both. And so, reader, do you. If ever you have looked on better days, if ever sat at any good man's feast—why then, reader, you have met Smiggers and known Blotton. If you are a Mason you know them intimately, and I feel that at Masonic Lodges Smiggers grandly presides and that Blotton is on guard against humbug, his old and permanent enemy.

Another man I know as well as if he were living to-day is the Cabman who drove Mr. Pickwick from St. Martin's-le-Grand to the Golden Cross: " 'Only a bob's vorth, Tommy,' cried the driver sulkily, for the information of his friend the waterman, as the cab drove off." I understand and sympathise, because I well know the look with which the taxi-driver who has been on the stand for a couple of hours receives my request to be driven from, say, His Majesty's Theatre to the Adelphi. Bless me, how beautifully Dickens conveys Mr. Pickwick's innocence by making him ask the age of the horse! Should I venture to ask an irritated taxi-driver the age or horse-power of whatever it is that has been standing on the rank for two hours? Dickens's enormous appreciation of Cockney wit is shown in the Cabman's answer. "Forty-two," being just conceivable, exactly hits off the Cockney's liking for exaggerated truth. Give your Cockney an inch and he will take an ell, and in the matter of Mr. Pickwick's credulity the Cabman's appetite grows with what it feeds on:

"And how long do you keep him out at a time?" inquired Mr. Pickwick, searching for further information.

"Two or three veeks," replied the man.

"Weeks!" said Mr. Pickwick in astonishment, and out came the note-book again.

"He lives at Pentonwil when he's at home," observed the driver coolly, "but we seldom takes him home, on account of his veakness."

"On account of his weakness!" reiterated the perplexed Mr. Pickwick.

"He always falls down when he's took out o' the cab," continued the driver, "but when he's in it, we bears him up werry tight, and takes him in werry short, so as he can't werry well fall down; and we've got a pair o' precious large wheels on, so ven he *does* move, they run after him, and he must go on—he can't help it."

Then again I perfectly know and understand the Red-headed Man who was working in his garden when Mr. Pickwick, Mr. Winkle, Mr. Tupman, Mr. Snodgrass, and the post-horse hove into view:

Mr. Pickwick called lustily, "Hollo there!"
The red-headed man raised his body, shaded his eyes with his hand, and stared, long and coolly, at Mr. Pickwick and his companions.
"Hollo there!" repeated Mr. Pickwick.
"Hollo!" was the red-headed man's reply.
"How far is it to Dingley Dell?"
"Better er seven mile."
"Is it a good road?"
"No, 'taint." Having uttered this brief reply, and apparently satisfied himself with another scrutiny, the red-headed man resumed his work.

This naturally brings me to the Long Gamekeeper with the Low Prophetic Voice:

"I never saw such a gun in my life," replied poor Mr. Winkle, looking at the lock, as if that would do any good. "It goes off of its own accord. It *will* do it."
"Will do it!" echoed Wardle, with something of irritation in his manner. "I wish it would kill something of its own accord."
"It'll do that afore long, sir," observed the tall man, in a low, prophetic voice.
"What do you mean by that observation, sir?" inquired Mr. Winkle, angrily.
"Never mind, sir, never mind," replied the long gamekeeper; "I've no family myself, sir; and this here boy's mother will get something handsome from Sir Geoffrey, if he's killed on his land. Load, again, sir, load again."

This in turn brings up Captain Boldwig, to whom I must always think that Kipling was indebted for his irascible Squire won over by McTurk:

Captain Boldwig was a little fierce man in a stiff black necker-chief and blue surtout, who, when he did condescend to walk about his property, did it in company with a thick rattan stick with a brass ferrule, and a gardener and sub-gardener with meek faces, to whom (the gardeners, not the stick) Captain Boldwig gave his orders with all due grandeur and ferocity; for Captain Boldwig's wife's sister had married a marquis, and the captain's house was a villa, and his land "grounds," and it was all very high, and mighty, and great.

Boldwig is of the same family as the Clubbers:

A great sensation was created throughout the room by the entrance of a tall gentleman in a blue coat and bright buttons, a large lady in blue satin, and two young ladies, on a similar scale, in fashionably-made dresses of the same hue.

"Commissioner—head of the yard—great man—remarkably great man," whispered the stranger in Mr. Tupman's ear, as the charitable committee ushered Sir Thomas Clubber and family to the top of the room. The Honourable Wilmot Snipe, and other distinguished gentlemen crowded to render homage to the Misses Clubber; and Sir Thomas Clubber stood bolt upright, and looked majestically over his black neckerchief at the assembled company.

"Mr. Smithie, Mrs. Smithie, and the Misses Smithie," was the next announcement.

"What's Mr. Smithie?" inquired Mr. Tracy Tupman.

"Something in the yard," replied the stranger. Mr. Smithie bowed deferentially to Sir Thomas Clubber; and Sir Thomas Clubber acknowledged the salute with conscious condescension. Lady Clubber took a telescopic view of Mrs. Smithie and family through her eye-glass, and Mrs. Smithie stared in her turn at Mrs. Somebody-else, whose husband was not in the dockyard at all.

The next arrivals, it will be remembered, are Colonel Bulder, Mrs. Colonel Bulder, and Miss Bulder who, of course, are the same class as the Clubbers and the Snipes. To this social stratum belong also Mr. Nupkins, Mrs. Nupkins, Miss Nupkins, and their dear friends the Porkenhams, including that dashing fellow and matrimonial catch Mr. Sidney Porkenham, the Griggses, and the Slummintowkens. But I am flying a little too high. My genuine friends in the Nupkins circle are Mr. Muzzle and the Cook. Yet I am not sure that I know even these quite so well as I know the still humbler members of this microcosm. "How many ladies are there?" asked Mr. Weller.

"Only two in our kitchen," said Mr. Muzzle; "cook and 'ousemaid. We keep a boy to do the dirty work, and a gal besides, but they dine in the wash'us."

"Oh, they dines in the wash'us, do they?" said Mr. Weller.

"Yes," replied Mr. Muzzle, "we tried 'em at our table when they first come, but we couldn't keep 'em. The gal's manners is dreadful vulgar; and the boy breathes so very hard while he's eating, that we found it impossible to sit at table with him."

"Young grampus!" said Mr. Weller.

"Oh, dreadful," rejoined Mr. Muzzle; "but that is the worst of country service, Mr. Weller; the juniors is always so very savage."

The juniors is always so very savage! This means that we are once more in that champaign of manners whose leading figure is Trabb's Boy. Yet I have a fancy that Trabb's Boy, when he grew up, lost something of his bright and shining quality. I feel that as the shades of the prison-house closed upon this glowing youth he became something totally different. Not, I think, a Roker, a Smangle, or a Mivins. But possibly a Smauker or even a Tuckle:

"Harris," said Mr. Tuckle, in a commanding tone.

"Sir," said the greengrocer.

"Have you got your gloves on?"

"Yes, sir."

"Then take the kiver off."

"Yes, sir."

The greengrocer did as he was told, with a show of great humility, and obsequiously handed Mr. Tuckle the carving-knife; in doing which, he accidentally gaped.

"What do you mean by that, sir?" said Mr. Tuckle, with great asperity.

"I beg your pardon, sir," replied the crestfallen greengrocer, "I didn't mean to do it, sir; I was up very late last night, sir."

"I tell you what my opinion of you is, Harris," said Mr. Tuckle, with a most impressive air, "you're a wulgar beast."

This is Trabb's Boy's "Don't know yah!" all over again. But with what a decline in meaning! From what Words-worthian heights has not Trabb's Boy fallen! I must quote another line or two for the sheer fun of it. Harris, asking pardon, has hoped that on the whole he gives satisfaction:

"No, you don't, sir," said Mr. Tuckle. "Very far from it, sir."

"We consider you an inattentive reskel," said the gentleman in the orange plush.

"And a low thief," added the gentleman in the green-foil smalls.

"And an unreclaimable blaygaird," added the gentleman in purple.

Is it too much to fancy that in the evening of their days these dandiacal ones are found reclining in the bosoms of Betsy Cluppins and Susannah Sanders? Sometimes I think their fate is less kindly and that they become the worser halves of Mrs. Mudberry which kept a mangle and Mrs. Bunkin which clear-starched. Certain it is that they were very much discussed at those parties in the Spaniards Tea-gardens whose presiding goddesses were Mrs. Bardell, Mrs. Rogers, and Mrs. Raddle which, as all the world knows, was Mrs. Cluppins's sister.

At this point there comes over me a surging sense of the hopelessness of my task. I appear to have cold-shouldered all sorts of people—Mr. Peter Magnus, whose friends were so easily amused, Mr. Dowler, arch-type of all the uxoriousness there ever has been or will be, Angelo Cyrus Bantam, Esquire, M.C. How Bantamesque is the latter's unimpugnable certainty! "We know you, Mr. Pickwick, we know you! You are the gentleman residing on Clapham Green

"who lost the use of his limbs from imprudently taking cold after port wine; who could not be moved in consequence of acute suffering, and who had the water from the king's bath bottled at one hundred and three degrees, and sent by wagon to his bedroom in town, where he bathed, sneezed, and the same day recovered. Very re-markable!"

It gives me a great deal of pleasure to administer the snub of omission to Mrs. Leo Hunter, though I should have liked room for Mrs. Pott, Rachel Wardle, and Miss Witherfield. But I sigh for the characters at that card-table —Lady Snuphanuph, Mrs. Colonel Wugsby, Miss Bolo! The reader will have remarked the almost Greek apposite-ness with which the two Miss Matinters "who, being single and singular, paid great court to the master of the cere-monies, in the hope of getting a stray partner now and then," remain wallflowers even in these belated pages. I see them as figures on a Pump Room tea-urn, still after a hundred years the unravished brides of quietness.

There are characters in this immortal work in whom, I confess with a certain shame, I have never been able to take a great deal of interest. I care singularly little for Mr. Perker, the Honourable Samuel Slumkey, and Horatio Fizkin, Esq., of Fizkin Lodge. While my heart aches for

Mr. Phunky, I positively dislike Sergeant Snubbin who lost Mr. Pickwick's case before he opened it. I am fond of Solomon Lucas, the Willie Clarkson of the period:

Equally humorous and agreeable was the appearance of Mr. Snodgrass in blue satin trunks and cloak, white silk tights and shoes, and Grecian helmet, which everybody knows (and if they do not, Mr. Solomon Lucas did) to have been the regular, authentic, everyday costume of a troubadour, from the earliest ages down to the time of their final disappearance from the face of the earth.

On the other hand, I have never been able to take to Solomon Pell. I do not love thee, Solomon Pell, the reason why I cannot tell; but this I know, and know full well, I do not love thee, Solomon Pell.

No! Not these considerable ones but the smaller, even the smallest deer have been my quarry. Ever since Messrs. Chapman and Hall extended their invitation I have been living once again with Samkin and Green's managing-clerk, Smithers and Price's chancery, and Pimkin and Thomas's out o' door, the last of whom, you remember, sings a capital song. I have been living with the Seidlitz-powder man, and the Gentleman who wore a brown coat and brass buttons, inky drabs and bluchers. With the Owner of the

ragged head, the sandy hair of which, scrupulously parted on one side, and flattened down with pomatum, was twisted into little semi-circular tails round a flat face ornamented with a pair of small eyes, and garnished with a very dirty shirt collar, and a rusty black stock.

With the Pot-boy, the Muffin Youth, and the Baked-potato Man. With the large-headed Young Man in a black wig, who brought with him to Bob Sawyer's party a

Scorbutic Youth in a long stock. With the Gentleman at the same party who wore a shirt emblazoned with pink anchors. With the Pale Youth of the plated watchguard. With the Prim Man in the cloth boots who had forgotten his anecdote but hoped he should manage to recollect it in the course of half an hour or so.

This last is, I feel, first cousin to the young man in Boswell, who would be witty bye-and-bye. "Bye-and-bye is easily said!" was a remark of Hamlet, with whom I began. Though bye-and-bye be stretched to cover the rest of time, it may be doubted whether ever again will be packed between the covers of one book such wit as Dickens was master of at twenty-five.